MEET ME
ON THE BRIDGE

MEET ME ON THE BRIDGE

NINE BRICKS TO CREATE STRONG
RELATIONSHIPS AT WORK

KIMBERLY SAUCEDA

NEW DEGREE PRESS
COPYRIGHT © 2022 KIMBERLY SAUCEDA
All rights reserved.

MEET ME ON THE BRIDGE
Nine Bricks to Create Strong Relationships at Work

ISBN		
	979-8-88504-524-7	*Paperback*
	979-8-88504-854-5	*Kindle Ebook*
	979-8-88504-530-8	*Ebook*

To my boys,
May you all be great at building bridges
Not only at work but also in life

Contents

	INTRODUCTION	11
CHAPTER 1.	THE CHANGE THAT HAPPENED (HOW WE GOT HERE)	21

PART 1.	**BUILDING THE FOUNDATION OF THE BRIDGE**	**37**
CHAPTER 2.	CORNERSTONE OF TRUST	43
CHAPTER 3.	PILLARS OF RESPECT	57
CHAPTER 4.	CREATING CONNECTION	73

PART 2.	**STRENGTHEN FOR HEALTHY RELATIONSHIPS**	**93**
CHAPTER 5.	SET EXPECTATIONS AND BOUNDARIES	97
CHAPTER 6.	GAIN ALIGNMENT	115
CHAPTER 7.	EXHIBIT BELIEF AND OPPORTUNITIES	129

PART 3.	**MAINTAIN (OR REBUILD) FOR THE LONG TERM**	**147**
CHAPTER 8.	CULTURE OF CURIOSITY	153

CHAPTER 9.	ACTIVELY LISTENING	167
CHAPTER 10.	OWNERSHIP WITH CONSISTENCY	179
PART 4.	**THE SEARCH FOR THE UNICORN:**	
	LEADERS WHO LEAD AND INSPIRE	**191**
CHAPTER 11.	LEADER #1 STEPHEN BOHNET	197
CHAPTER 12.	LEADER #2 KRISTA TODD	207
CHAPTER 13.	LEADER #3 RODNEY TOY	217
CHAPTER 14.	FINAL THOUGHTS	227
	ACKNOWLEDGMENTS	235
	APPENDIX	243

"Alone we can do so little. Together we can do so much."

~HELEN KELLER

Introduction

"I'm here to build a bridge. Kachink, kachink, kachink. *Ding!* That's my hammer as I work on building this bridge connecting us," I said to my son as I made a motion like hammering a nail.

Bridges create a way to go from one side to another. In this case, I wanted to create a way for us to be closer without it being one-sided work for either of us. My hope was that we would each work to move closer to the other.

He would work on his side, and I would work on my side. We'd meet together in the middle of the bridge.

Daily intentional interactions build a bridge, brick by brick. (While the bridge analogy with my son was one of wood planks, nails, and hammers, the analogy for this book will use bricks.)

I believe this is exactly how it is in business. Every day, both sides are choosing actions and words that will strengthen the bond between the manager and the employee. Whether you are reading this as a manager or as an employee, you are either actively building the bridge in everything you do or you're not.

My invitation to you is: *Meet Me on the Bridge.*

~ ~ ~ ~

In May 2020, when the pandemic was still new and we were figuring things out, my sons, fourteen and eleven years old at the time, started spending a lot of time in their rooms—for Zoom classes and just to have some time away from other members of the family.

One morning, I walked into Andrew's room (my oldest), navigating baseball cleats, gray sweats, and other random bits of clothes. While he's very smart and athletic, his room looks like his dresser and closet may have exploded.

He was sitting at his desk, deep in thought, with his chestnut brown hair falling onto his forehead.

"Hi, friend," I started as I kissed his forehead. "How are you?"

"I'm good, Mom. What's up?"

"I'm coming in to see how things are. This is a strange world these days. I want to know how you are," I continued.

I explained how I intended to come in every morning and talk with him to build a bridge—not to find out how his grades were or to find out if his room was clean. I explained I wanted to create a bridge for us to have a solid relationship.

"Thanks, Mom," he replied with a smile before returning to his English assignment.

Every day, in every way, you're building a bridge with everyone. You're either doing things to reinforce the bridge (following through on what you say, building trust, actively listening, etc.) or the bridge is decaying and deteriorating. This is what happens when a structure is left alone without maintenance. In some cases, if you do something against how you want to be in the relationship, you can blow up the bridge.

After a few days of me visiting him for a chat each morning, Andrew came into my office early one day before I had gone to see him, smiling broadly.

"Hi, friend, kachink, kachink, kachink. *Ding*! I'm here to build a bridge. How is your day going?" he said.

Seeing him in the doorway made me so happy. I had not expected him to come to me.

We talked about how things were going for each of us—the schoolwork he had, the friends he was making (even with remote classes), and my work. We spent time connecting and finding out more about each other. We were truly listening to each other. We both now looked forward to and enjoyed our time together. We were investing time daily in our relationship and making it much stronger.

"I really like our bridge," he said with a smile.

I did too.

That's the thing about building the bridge. It must be two people coming together. Both sides must build the bridge together. If not, it is merely a lookout. I loved that he understood this and was doing his part to build his side.

EVERY DAY, WE CAN BUILD A BRIDGE TO CREATE A STRONGER RELATIONSHIP, BRICK BY BRICK

This analogy translates well into the corporate world. There are two sides to the potential bridge—the employee and the manager.

Interestingly, through conversations, research, and my own experience with managers and coworkers in corporations, I found some people think the responsibility of the relationship in business is on the manager or the employee. There are shelves and shelves of books written about one side (how to be a great manager) or the other (how to be a great employee).

What if the key is for both sides to be bridge builders?

I personally have experience on both sides—as an employee and as a manager. Early in my career, I was an employee at Clorox and Nestle in Consumer Insights. Then I transitioned into technology companies and worked at Plantronics in a hybrid product marketing/product management role and later at Apple on iPhone Product Marketing to launch iPhone 6 and 6s.

As a manager of teams, I led the marketing team at a start-up and then led the Smart Home Marketing team at Logitech. In each experience, I worked to build strong teams that performed well. The Smart Home Marketing team became a valued voice at the table. The successes were due to creating solid bonds with the team.

The strongest work relationships I experienced (both as a manager and as an employee) were when both sides worked on the relationship and met each other on the bridge.

The relationship is lopsided if you are not both working on building the bridge. Think back to a time when you put forth the effort or gave more of yourself. Was it reciprocated? It is hard to respect someone if they are not respecting you. It is challenging to try and communicate with someone if they are not willing to have an open dialogue. These are just some of the bricks necessary to build the bridge.

Now consider the other side.

Think of a time in your career when your manager was all in for you. How did you show up for them? Or when an employee was consistently going the extra mile, how did you respond in turn as the manager?

In July 2008, I began working at Palm, the company that created the Palm Pilot and personal digital assistants (PDAs). They created one of the first smartphones, and it had a touchscreen. If we go back in time, this was at the end of the Centro era (smartphone with a touchscreen and keyboard) and just before the new highly-anticipated *Pre* came to market.

They touted the Pre as a device that would potentially rival the recently launched iPhone, which was gaining incredible momentum.

Initially, I worked under the Centro product line manager, who went out on medical leave a few weeks after I started. So, for a while, I reported to the Director of Product Management, Stephane. He pulled me into his office to explain that since my manager was on medical leave, I would need to step up and cover his role for an undetermined amount of time until he returned.

"Kimberly, we have to find a way to stretch sales of Centro until we can launch Pre next spring. Find a way to work with marketing and breathe some extra life into this line over the holidays. You're in charge of a tiger team to make this happen."

I was elated. First, I had the pleasure of working with an incredibly talented marketer, Caitlin. We had so much fun brainstorming ideas. Our meetings felt so synergistic. She would start an idea, and then I would build on it. Or I would begin, and she would build on it. The meetings were lighthearted, fun, and full of laughter. We came up with new ways to ignite the market.

In retrospect, we worked together so well because Caitlin and I cocreated this environment of mutual respect, trust, and connection. I learned a great deal about marketing by working so closely with her for several weeks. She effortlessly demonstrated incredible bridge building.

Second, with a small team of operations, finance, demand, and a few colleagues, we created a pricing plan to address the challenges we had been facing and target new and existing customers, which led to the leeway we needed.

Each week, I presented to Ed Colligan, one of the best CEOs I have ever worked for. Still, it felt a bit daunting to provide updates on a critical initiative, only having been at the company less than two months. The trust and belief Stephane (the director and my interim boss) had in me propelled me to step up into this role. He provided me with the right balance of guidance, coaching, and feedback.

Two years later, when I was managing my team, I remembered all of this. I worked hard to create opportunities to let my team shine. I would highlight their accomplishments to management. At a meeting with the board of directors, I highlighted the social media manager for her innovative campaign that was building our community. After that, she had more and more ideas about how to increase the audience. At the next meeting, I asked her to present her ideas for the next campaign, which helped grow her comfort level in presenting to executives. She stepped up and exceeded the CEO's expectations.

When you are all in for your employees, they excel. They want to be the potential you see in them. In some ways, it is a self-fulfilling prophecy.

These kinds of positive working relationships between managers and employees are the ones we seek to emulate. We need to know what bricks to use for our bridges to do so.

Based on dozens of interviews with business professionals and authors and much research, certain bricks stand out as key ingredients to building a solid bridge.

NINE BRICKS TO BUILD A SOLID BRIDGE AT WORK
- Cornerstone of Trust
- Pillars of Respect
- Creating Connection
- Set Expectations and Boundaries
- Gain Alignment
- Exhibit Belief and Development
- Culture of Curiosity
- Actively Listening
- Ownership with Consistency

With these bricks, you can build a solid bridge with a two-way path that both manager and employee can cross.

FOCUS FOR MANAGERS
Understanding each other's strengths and leaning into them helps strengthen the bridge. Explore the aspirations, values, and interests of your employees. In doing this, you not only uncover what is important to them but how to move beyond motivating them to inspiring them. This can strengthen the connection as well as the respect and trust you both have in each other.

The key to leading is not *one size fits all*, which does not serve anyone. It is *one size fits you*. Craft a style of leading that is personalized to you and fits your employees (and their individual needs).

FOCUS FOR EMPLOYEES

Both sides need to strengthen the bridge with their interactions. Employees can do this by understanding their manager (in the same way we talked about the manager seeking to understand the employee). This will also engender a deeper connection, more trust, and more respect for each other.

By doing this, you achieve incredible results. When a manager sees the employee's greatness and possibility, that person steps up, shines, and wants to excel in their role. Think back to when someone has believed in what you can become. How did you show up for them? In my experience, this is when I (and my employees for me) have risen to the occasion and exceeded expectations.

~ ~ ~ ~

Bridge building is accomplished brick by brick, intentionally through consistent action and words. This does not happen overnight. While big actions and/or beautiful speeches about intentions can be very impactful, this happens through the consistency in how the bridge is built and maintained.

This book lays out the bricks to create a solid relationship at work. While this book is primarily focused on employees and managers, you can create strong relationships with everyone you work with by leveraging these bricks. With the stories and research included throughout this book, you will see what works and what does not to support you as you create, maintain, rebuild, and overall solidify your bridges.

CHAPTER 1:

The Change That Happened (How We Got Here)

"Each time you learn something new you must readjust the whole framework of your knowledge."

~ELEANOR ROOSEVELT

"I quit."

Across the nation, people aren't just saying that phrase. They're doing it at record-breaking rates.

In November 2021, a record 4.5 million workers left their jobs, according to the US Department of Labor's latest Job Openings and Labor Turnover report. According to a Bankrate survey in late 2021, 55 percent of people said they were going to look for a new job in 2022. Then 4.3 million workers quit in January 2022, according to *CNBC* reporting on the US Department of Labor's Job Openings and Labor Turnover.

**THE PANDEMIC HAS CHANGED HOW
PEOPLE THINK ABOUT THEIR JOBS**

According to an *INC Magazine* article from August 2021, the Great Resignation is a term first coined in 2019 by Texas A&M's Anthony Klotz to predict a mass, voluntary exodus from the workforce. Some have also dubbed this trend the Great Rethink.

With this ongoing trend in which employees have voluntarily resigned *en masse* since early 2021, we have seen a cultural shift. Employees do not want to go back to what they had known—long hours, in-person work five days a week, and the lack of flexibility. Many are talking about this in terms of flexibility of hours and working from home.

According to a 2021 Gallup poll of thirteen thousand employees, below are the most important factors in their next job (Barry, 2022):

Most Important Factors for Employees When Considering a New Job, by Gender			
% Very Important			
Women		Men	
Greater work-life balance and better well-being	66%	Increases income and improved benefits	63%
Increases income and improved benefits	65%	Greater work-life balance and better well-being	56%
Allows me to do what I do best	62%	Allows me to do what I do best	53%
Provides greater stability and job security	54%	Provides greater stability and job security	52%
Organization is diverse and inclusive	52%	COVID-19 vaccine policies align with my beliefs	39%

From the table above, we see both men and women mostly view the same factors as important when considering a new job. Women, however, want more diversity and inclusion in the organization. Both want great work-life balance, better well-being, and a position that allows them to do what they do best. Managers can influence the majority of these factors.

Providing more insight into what's driving the Great Resignation, Mark Crowley, from Fast Company, chatted with Gallup's chief research scientist, Jim Harter, in a March 2022 article to understand the factors, in addition to a paycheck, that caused people to quit. Here are some highlights:

- Sixty-four percent of job seekers say the desire to earn more money is an important driver of the job search

- Two-thirds of the reasons people left jobs in 2021 were because of issues related to engagement and overall well-being, according to Harter

- Forty-two percent cited reasons tied to how they feel about their bosses and organizational cultures

- Twenty-one percent of the reasons centered on well-being: employees' feelings about their work-life balance, work schedules, and their ability to work remotely some of the time

- Employees who are struggling (anyone on the Gallup poll of well-being that scores five to six) or suffering (score of four or lower) have two times the amount of turnover

"Leaders need a realization that building a culture that improves lives will be required to attract and retain great people," Harter says. "There's a huge gap today between knowing this and getting it done."

IRON SHARPENS IRON: STRONGER MANAGERS LEAD TO STRONG EMPLOYEES

In fact, Steve Tadelis, an economics professor at UC Berkeley's Haas School of Business, noted during a 2022 *Freakonomics* podcast episode titled "Why Are There So Many Bad Bosses" that having a good boss is associated with an attrition drop of about 60 percent. Additionally, he added:

What we see then is that managers help retain better employees more than worse employees, which shows that the impact of being a better manager is strongest where it matters the most.

It is important that we create this strong relationship between both manager and employee.

In December 2021, the online job site *Indeed* released the results of a survey of one thousand workers who left at least two jobs since March 2020 (Birt, 2021). Of those respondents, 92 percent said:

The pandemic made them feel life is too short to stay in a job they weren't passionate about.

I have heard this from those I interviewed as well. We spend so much time at work that we should be enjoying it.

During the pandemic, the amount of time at work has increased, as people have been working longer hours.

According to data from the business support company NordVPN Teams published in *The Guardian*, the average length of time that an employee working from home in the UK, Austria, Canada, and the US is logged on at their computer increased by more than two hours a day since the pandemic began in March 2020. In the US, employees worked eight hours a day online (prepandemic), and the number of hours worked moved up to eleven hours in 2021.

Prior to the pandemic, some rough boundaries existed. You would leave work and drive home. For many, that was a time to unwind, decompress, and shift from work thoughts to focus on home. That said, I know for some people, the line was blurry even before the pandemic, meaning that quite often, after dinner, they would log on to their work computer to do additional work at home.

Since there was no commute from work to home during the pandemic, for all intents and purposes, the previously blurry boundaries between work and personal life were completely erased. Bedrooms turned into offices, and everyone was now at home all day.

My coaching clients would say, "It is so hard to turn my work brain off. My computer is right there. I think, 'Just a quick check of my email…' But then two hours later and I'm still mired in it."

With the extra time that people have without the commute, additional meetings were tacked on to the day, which is the reason that the workday went from eight to eleven hours in 2021.

These extra work hours lead to burnout, which is defined as a psychological syndrome emerging as a prolonged response to chronic interpersonal stressors on the job, according to Christina Maslach and Michael P. Leiter in their 2016 "Understanding the burnout experience: recent research and its implications for psychiatry" article published in *World Psychiatry*.

In 2021, the website *Indeed* surveyed fifteen hundred US workers of various age groups, across many industries and levels, and found employee burnout increased from 2020 to 2021 (Threlkeld, 2021). Over half (52 percent) of respondents noted that they felt burned out compared to 43 percent in the pre-COVID survey.

Looking at the data by generation, the findings are the same, with each generation seeing an increase. Gen Z and millennials are the most affected at 58 percent and 59 percent reporting burnout, respectively. (Pew Research Center defines millennials as those born between 1981–1996 and Gen Z as those born between 1997–2012, according to their 2019 article, "Defining generations: Where millennials end and Generation Z begins.")

Of all of those surveyed, 67 percent believe burnout worsened over the pandemic. According to this same survey, 27 percent of all respondents are unable to unplug from work. This also explains the burnout.

Not all companies agree on the solution for burnout. Some have incorporated mental health benefits, such as Headspace (a meditation app) or an extra week off work. These actions can be seen as looking at the symptom and not at the cause.

Simply offering these perks doesn't solve the problem, according to Jennifer Moss, author of *The Burnout Epidemic: The Rise of Chronic Stress and How We Can Fix It*. Employers still expect employees to produce as much or more than prepandemic. The organization's expectations of work have not changed. Having a week off simply means you come back to a mountain of work, which Moss found increases the employee's stress during a week off to "de-stress."

She suggests weekly check-ins between a manager and an employee that are not related to work to see how the employee is doing. Managers and employees can craft the balance that each of them needs.

According to Moss's 2019 *Harvard Business Review* article citing Stanford research, burnout costs $190 million annually because of declines in productivity, lower employee engagement, absenteeism, lower organizational commitment, and turnover.

There are health implications from overwork as well.

From a recent World Health Organization (WHO) study, the findings are very concerning:

- Overwork is the single most significant risk factor for occupational disease (defined as an illness associated with a particular occupation or industry)

- Working more than fifty-five hours a week increases the risk of stroke by 35 percent and 17 percent higher risk for heart disease compared to those who work thirty-five to forty hours

- Overwork has significant negative ripple effects on health and behavior—including poor sleep, inadequate exercise, unhealthy diet, smoking, and excessive drinking

It is no wonder people are reconsidering what they want the role of work to be in their lives.

As mentioned earlier, there have been many different names for this time of people quitting: the Great Resignation, Great Reshuffle, or Great Realization. What if this is the Great Reimagination of work? We (both employees and managers) have learned so much over the past few years. We need to adjust our framework.

> *"Each time you learn something new, you must readjust the whole framework of your knowledge."*
>
> ~ELEANOR ROOSEVELT

Employees know more about what they want in their job. As noted above, both women and men want better well-being and want to do their best at work. Managers have been learning new ways to manage in the remote world. Coming together to understand what both sides want and need creates a strong relationship.

WITHOUT COMING TOGETHER, THE BRIDGE WILL FALL
We've all heard people leave their boss, not the company.

Let's break this down by some numbers:

A Gallup poll published in *Fortune Magazine* in 2015 concluded the number one reason people quit their jobs is a bad boss or immediate supervisor (Snyder, 2015). According to a 2020 SHRM (Society for Human Resource Management) survey, 84 percent of American workers say poorly trained people managers create a lot of unnecessary work and stress. We also saw that a great manager could significantly influence retention.

Let's look at the cost of this:

US companies lost an estimated $223 billion due to culture-caused turnover, according to a SHRM 2019 Q3 survey.

This turnover has more than financial considerations. Finding new talent requires time and current resources (for both sourcing and interviewing). Additionally, a new employee takes time to ramp up in a new position and understand the company culture.

EMPLOYEE ENGAGEMENT DECLINED IN 2021

According to the 2022 Gallup article "US Employee Engagement Drops for First Year in a Decade," citing Gallup's State of the Global Workplace, only 34 percent of US employees in 2021 were engaged in the workplace (Harter, 2022). (Gallup defines engagement as "the involvement and enthusiasm of employees in both their work and workplace.") This is the first drop in employee engagement in a decade. Findings in this same survey indicate that the main drivers for this decline were the following:

- Clarity of expectations
- Having the right materials and equipment
- Opportunity for workers to do what they do best

Manager engagement is also on the decline while burnout is on the rise. This same Gallup article recommends two managerial-level changes that could help increase overall employee engagement. Managers need to be continually developing in their work.

According to Jim Harter of Gallup, managers also need to have "coaching conversations with *their* manager—just as the expectation with managers to do with their employees. It is almost impossible to engage your employees if managers themselves are burned out and not engaged."

Again, part of this burnout needs to be fixed by the organization. Adding more and more to do as well as increasing the amount of time spent in meetings becomes too much. Employees and managers can help alleviate this with discussion and implementation of boundaries.

THOSE WHO FEEL HEARD ARE 4.6 TIMES MORE LIKELY TO PERFORM AT THEIR BEST

In a September 2019 article in *INC Magazine*, Melanie Curtin cited Salesforce Research, which surveyed over fifteen hundred business professionals on values-driven leadership and workplace equality. They found a surprisingly high statistic.

"When an employee feels heard, that person is 4.6 times more likely to feel empowered to perform to the best of their abilities."

As a manager, this should be of critical importance. The next question, then, is how you help someone feel heard. We explore this in the Actively Listening chapter, where we talk about the three levels of listening.

While people received feedback more frequently during the pandemic, according to a Gallup poll of employees (45 percent say they received feedback daily or a few times a week in 2020 versus only 26 percent in 2019), the feedback they received was not actionable or helpful. Gallup notes that receiving meaningful feedback is a critical factor for employee engagement (Harter, 2021).

I recently interviewed Watermark CEO Peggy Northrop about the keys to thriving in the new world of work. During our talk, she quoted author Rob Cross, who said:

The constant small interactions we make with others are so important now.

According to Northrop, managers have new responsibilities. They need to look out for the whole person, including their mental well-being. This entails creating better connections with them, so they have trust and respect. It is also giving better feedback with an understanding of the other person.

We'll explore all of these as we look at how to build the bridge from both sides.

Previously, managers expected employees to be productive and efficient—without emotion—and that they (managers) would do the same. Northrop noted that now managers need to show some vulnerability and connect with their employees. Managers also need to be okay with employees showing up as vulnerable.

This sea change is similar to what has been happening with Diversity, Equity, and Inclusion (DEI). Companies realize and research confirms that more diverse leadership performs better and is stronger with diverse opinions. We see that when companies embrace people bringing their authentic selves to work, including their emotions, there is less turnover and better results.

McKinsey's 2020 report, "Diversity Wins: How Inclusion Matters," shows organizations with a diversity of gender are 25 percent more likely to be more profitable than their peers. This report also shows organizations with a diversity of ethnicity are 36 percent more likely to be more profitable than their peers.

According to a February 2022 Entrepreneur article, the World Economic Forum's report "Diversity, Equity, and Inclusion 4.0" suggests companies with diverse employees have "up to

20 percent higher rate of innovation and 19 percent higher innovation revenues."

From the same SHRM study as above, here are the five people skills employees would like to see managers improve on:

- Communicating effectively (41 percent)
- Developing and training the team (38 percent)
- Managing time and delegating (37 percent)
- Cultivating a positive and inclusive team culture (35 percent)
- Managing team performance (35 percent)

In the Introduction, we talked about how important it is to create a strong relationship between employee and manager when building a bridge. We'll do that by having each of these people skills be a *brick* in the bridge.

While I agree that quite often, people are promoted to a management position and then do not receive the proper training to become great managers, this book will look at the relationship between the manager and the employee. It is too easy to point the finger at the manager solely. The relationship is a two-way street.

OUTCOMES, NOT RESULTS

For the longest time, there was a mentality that you need to be in the office to be productive. The world has now seen it is more than possible to still be productive while working at home. That said, employees want to have a different measurement than just results.

A recent 2021 survey published by *Harvard Business Review* in the article "What Your Future Employees Want Most" found people want to be measured differently:

Eighty-six percent of employees said they would prefer to work for a company that prioritizes outcomes over output.

Even with more employees working from home, managers still play a critical role in an employee's experience at work.

According to the *Harvard Business Review* article, "11 Trends that Will Shape Work in 2022 and Beyond:"

The manager-employee relationship has become more important than ever. For hybrid and remote employees, their managers are the primary connection through which they experience their employer. Managers are also the first line in surfacing and elevating fairness concerns and can make the difference between a highly public walkout or a cocreated solution to employee concerns.

The key part needs to be a solid relationship between a manager and an employee.

So much has changed over the past few years. Moving forward and building strong relationships is going to be important to thriving in work, whether hybrid, remote, or in person. It can no longer just be about results. Strong relationships enable great results, which are seen when there is a sturdy bridge between both sides.

In the following chapters, we will walk through the bricks needed to build the foundation of the bridge (trust, respect, and connection). We will also explore the bricks needed to maintain the bridge to keep a solid relationship, as well as the bricks to rebuild the bridge if it has been damaged, which sometimes happens with relationships.

PART 1:

BUILDING THE FOUNDATION OF THE BRIDGE

In the next three chapters, we'll learn about trust, respect, and connection through stories and research. These three core bricks are needed to create a solid foundation for the bridge.

It is important to start with these bricks to ensure you have a solid foundation for your relationship. We want the relationship to be so strong that it can withstand the inevitable bumps that occasionally happen when people work together.

CORNERSTONE OF TRUST
With trust, we will see that it is, in fact, learnable and how much trust strengthens the relationship when it is present. Establishing trust pays dividends in numerous ways, including higher productivity. Without trust, we are less productive, and there is more friction in the relationship. Starting here provides the cornerstone of the foundation.

PILLARS OF RESPECT
The two types of respect to focus on are: owed and earned. We will explore the challenges of not having respect. This is where we will also talk about creating an inclusive space where both sides can show up fully and authentically.

Because there are so many challenges if you do not have trust and respect solidly in place, these are the two you must build first. You can, and often will, continue to build more trust and respect as you are creating connection, the next brick.

CREATING CONNECTION
With connection, we'll see this is an integral piece of the relationship. Creating a connection between an employee and manager enables a deeper understanding of each other. This connection also moves the relationship from transactional to one that is multifaceted and more meaningful.

From my twenty years of experience in the corporate world, working across organizations such as Apple and Nestle, I have seen how important it is to build trust, respect, and connection. Having this trifecta in place creates a relationship where each person cares about the other and their well-being. Having a relationship that is not purely transactional creates more engagement on both sides. As an employee, I wanted to overdeliver for the managers with whom I had a solid relationship, and I did. It was more of a slog to work for the managers with whom a poor relationship existed.

This is how you can transform the relationship.

Because of that, an interviewer and interviewee can create this foundation even during the hiring stage. During this process, they are getting to know each other as manager and prospective employee. This can be an excellent opportunity to build trust, respect, and connection. These can also easily be built during the first few weeks of getting to know each other if one is intentional with their actions.

Align your words and actions on both ends. Without this, there is a lack of clarity and consistency, which leads to destroying the trust, respect, and connection you are trying to build.

When these three elements are sturdy and solid, they will support the relationship through storms and conflict. To do that, they must be continually and intentionally tended. This does not necessarily mean big gestures each day but rather demonstrating through small interactions on a regular basis. In doing that, the relationship continues to strengthen.

From this foundation, you can then layer in the other bricks to strengthen and maintain the bridge.

If the bridge becomes damaged or destroyed, come back to the three original bricks of trust, respect, and connection. As the foundation's bricks, you need these to be sturdy to ensure that your relationship remains strong.

At the end of each chapter, there are tips for the manager as well as tips for the employee. These draw from my experiences as a manager and as an employee, my experiences coaching clients and teams, and the dozens of interviews and research conducted for this book. While these mostly focus on the manager-employee relationship, we can extend many of these out to the full team.

CHAPTER 2:

Cornerstone of Trust

"Trust is like the air we breathe. When it's present, nobody really notices. When it's absent, everybody notices."

~WARREN BUFFETT

Many believe trust is something you work on once, if needed, and then the one time should be enough. They assume trust then just exists, with no need to maintain it. I believe trust is the bedrock for the bridge and needs constant reinforcement through daily interactions, both big and small.

Bedrock is the fundamental principle(s) upon which a sound foundation is based.

Geologists refer to bedrock as the compacted rock that sits below the surface of the soil. In the real world, bedrock is hard and sometimes breakable, just as trust is the bedrock in a relationship and can atrophy. We anchor most large buildings into the bedrock with structures called *foundations*.

Without trust, your bridge will not anchor into a solid foundation.

Trust is a belief in the reliability, truth, ability, or strength of someone or something. With trust, both sides need to be open, clearly communicate expectations, and provide the space for your employee (or manager) to achieve the expectations.

Of the sixteen managers I had in my twenty years in marketing, Marti was the most challenging. Interestingly, we were coworkers before she was my boss. As coworkers, we worked well together on launches.

That said, she could be a bit caustic, like a bull in a China shop, when she wanted something to get done and felt like people were not seeing it her way. In numerous meetings, I would stay behind to talk to the packaging team and *reinterpret* what she had said, as they felt incredibly frustrated. At the moment, I didn't mind. We had the same goal. We both wanted to deliver a phenomenal launch.

That all changed a few months later when I received my annual review.

Since kindergarten, I have received "works well with others" on every performance assessment.

So, I was shocked to find out I received "needs improvement" on working with others during my annual review, just a few weeks after Marti had received her promotion. I will never know why, but I later learned from a coworker she had provided inaccurate information to our manager about my performance.

A few months later, she called me into her office and closed the door.

"Kimberly, I'm not sure what you're doing on this launch now. You claim to have launched products before. I'm now not sure you've ever actually launched a product successfully," she said.

It was at that moment I realized two truths:

1. She did not have trust in me or my marketing or product management skills.

2. I completely lost respect for her. We had worked together on a prior launch that had been a blockbuster. She was patently incorrect about my product marketing and launch skills. (We will cover respect in the next chapter.)

From that point on, she nitpicked all the details in each part of my work. Her comments were often snide or snarky when it was just the two of us. During presentations, she would break in and talk over me, making it seem like she did not trust I would cover all the points accurately.

Even when I performed above and beyond and had other teams telling her I was doing an exceptional job, the trust was never there on her end. I eventually had to accept that sometimes managers will not trust you no matter what you do. This is not necessarily a reflection of you but is sometimes a flaw or a misstep in training or not training managers.

I have always believed in building bridges.

If the other person (my manager, in this case) is unwilling to build their part of the bridge, it is only a lookout.

You cannot build the bridge to someone else if they will not build their side. What I learned from this is how critical trust (and respect) are for the bridge.

Sometimes invaluable lessons come from the most challenging circumstances. I decided I wanted to be the opposite kind of manager from Marti, as the relationship was so debilitating for me. As a manager, I lifted up my team and worked to highlight them to upper management. I found opportunities for them to develop and grow. I respected their perspectives and listened openly to their opinions. I set clear expectations so they would know what the goals were and how to achieve them.

This quote from Michelle Obama inspired me:

Always stay true to who you are and do not let what others say about you distract you from your goals.

My goal was and is to create healthy, high-performing teams. The first step is to trust the team.

==What if trust is first given by you and then the recipient (in this case, your team) proves over time they are worthy of that trust?==

This may feel like a radical approach at first, but it is important.

Stephen M.R. Covey, author of three books on trust, including *Trust and Inspire: How Truly Great Leaders Unleash Greatness in Others,* is an expert on the subject. In this 2022 book, he discusses two types of managers: *Command and Control* managers and *Trust and Inspire* managers.

One of the main differences Covey described is Command and Control people are trying to manage people the same way they manage things. He said:

... when you try to manage people like you manage things, you deny the very qualities people possess that bring real, unique value and enable them to solve problems and make sedition in creative, productive ways outside of how you might.

With Command and Control, the manager focuses on efficiency. They work from a place of position and power. The relationship is transactional, with managers looking at employees as resources to get things done, which means managers attain compliance and not much more. Employees will coordinate with each other to accomplish tasks, not collaborate.

This style has begun to improve over time by adding in emotional intelligence, a focus on perks for employees, and motivating employees. Perks are interesting because the focus is on productivity for the employee, not necessarily happier employees, as Covey points out. Even adding these pieces is not enough. This manager motivates but does not inspire. This style is only a kinder version of Command and Control.

In contrast, the Trust and Inspire leader ignites the employees' passions, which inspires and engages them. Instead of micromanaging, these leaders empower their teams while creating guidelines and accountability. These managers focus on the effectiveness of their employees, not efficiency. Employees move beyond coordination to collaboration.

In trusting people to do a great job (and believing in what they can become and achieve, which we will cover in another chapter) you inspire them to perform at their fullest potential.

IS TRUST LEARNABLE?
In *The Speed of Trust: The One Thing that Changes Everything*, Covey posits that trust, a crucial skill, is learnable:

Trust is the number one competency because it makes you better at every other thing that you need to do.

This is exactly why we begin with trust for our bridge.

This quote is from Covey's speaking engagement at LEAD in 2016, where he talked about trust, how its presence can improve business, how its lack can make business more challenging, and the components needed to create trust. In that talk and his book, he discusses a low trust tax and a high trust dividend. The *tax* occurs when there is low trust because the speed goes down and the cost goes up, meaning it takes longer to accomplish a task when trust is low with the person you are working with.

The communication is not as smooth and easy. Think about interactions where you do not have trust. You feel like you need to double-check things. You want to confirm the other person will follow through on the commitment. Low trust taxes cause the interaction to take longer.

When there is high trust, you have a "dividend." If you think of a situation when you had high trust at work, it was likely a situation where things ran smoothly and much more easily. You don't spend as much time explaining things. When someone says they will do something, you believe they will because you trust them. You both can accomplish work faster and easier.

This was the case for me when I worked on a small cross-functional team to complete a critical, time-sensitive program at Palm. We had such high trust in one another that we would turn deliverables around in a week. We had quick meetings to give a status update, identify challenges, craft a solution, and then each person would execute their given task. Because we knew we could rely on each other, there were no long discussions about how each person would do something. The team was a well-oiled, effective machine and highly collaborative.

In his September 2021 article in *Inc Magazine*, Covey doubled down on the importance of trust.

Trust makes it easier for executives to achieve most business goals. If employees and customers believe what you're saying, they're much more likely to follow your lead. Trust builds goodwill.

That goodwill builds this bridge.

TRUST IS BELIEF IN YOUR TEAM

At a major retailer, Lynn worked as a PR manager. She was overseeing the announcement of a massive organizational change. Given the scope, everyone, including Lynn, worked hard to ensure everything was correct. Under a deadline to make the announcement, Lynn received edits from others and incorporated them as quickly as possible. Then she would resend the announcement, as was customary, to her stakeholders.

Her manager, Mike, in a mix of stress and anxiety about the announcement, was impatient while waiting for its finalization. He decided to call her.

"Are you done with the announcement?" he asked with an exasperated sigh to punctuate his frustration.

"Not quite. Will let you know," she replied before giving him more information on the status of the announcement and then hanging up the phone.

Five minutes later, he called again. "Are you done yet?"

This phone call with the same question came every five minutes.

Lynn incorporated the changes from others and worked to refine the document to send it out again. Like a pot boiling over with water, Lynn could not handle any more. The next time he called, she yelled at him.

"If you don't stop calling me, I will never get this done!" Lynn yelled.

This was not a great bridge-building interaction on either side. Because other people heard her, Mike was embarrassed, which quickly turned to anger. Lynn was incredibly frustrated that Mike did not trust her to do her job and felt the need to check in every few minutes.

Trust needs to be consistent.

Lynn had been delivering on all her projects. Second-guessing her was not helping Mike achieve what he wanted—to get the announcement out sooner.

While yelling at Mike may not have been the best reaction, this action illustrates the low trust tax.

~ ~ ~ ~

A 2017 study published in the *Harvard Business Review*, shows considerable differences in how people feel and perform in relation to the level of trust at their company. Compared with people at low trust companies, people at high-trust companies report:

- 74 percent less stress
- 106 percent more energy at work
- 13 percent fewer sick days
- 40 percent less burnout
- 29 percent more satisfaction with their lives
- 50 percent higher productivity
- 76 percent more engagement

Imagine if you had employees who experienced much less stress and had more energy at work. What would it be like to have nearly 80 percent engagement overall with your employees? That would be a very happy, healthy team.

Building trust begins with both the manager and the employee. It is something that needs tending to each day.

BECOME THE PERSON THEY TURN TO
Though Arianna was fairly new to the consulting world, she was a quick learner. As an analyst at one of the big three consulting firms in the US, Arianna was driven and dove into every project she received. She wanted to understand all of the parts of each project and the partner companies.

Late one afternoon, her manager, Stephanie, saw Arianna and stopped her.

"Hey, walk with me. I want you to join this call," she said.

This was quite unusual. Arianna followed her down the hallway. Stephanie told her she would be there only to observe how things went. In the conference room, Arianna intently listened as they walked through a contract with a new company they were onboarding.

A week later, Stephanie came by Arianna's desk to ask her to attend another meeting.

"Come in and sit and listen in on this call. We're going to cover fees today. The CFO is going to be there. It will be a great learning opportunity for you."

Each time, Arianna learned more about the business and how it worked.

Stephanie continued to bring Arianna into more projects and have her help earlier on them. With each interaction, the scope of Arianna's work increased. She built on the initial trust each day. Arianna learned when to speak up and when to wait to voice her thoughts privately with Stephanie.

Soon, Stephanie had Arianna take on even more projects and have even more ownership. Over time, they built a solid relationship. If Stephanie needed to be away for an afternoon, she knew she could count on Arianna to take care of the projects. Stephanie saw potential in Arianna early on with her leadership skills, and she wanted to grow these skills in Arianna.

Arianna remembers the trust Stephanie placed in her from the very start, and that has stuck with her.

Now the CEO of her own company, Arianna considers trust to be vital to her organization. She hires smart people to head up the teams. She brings them into the conversations early and then trusts them to execute on their deliverables. During the pandemic, her team had daily stand-ups. In doing so, people stayed connected, and the team addressed issues in a timely manner. She appreciates the trust Stephanie placed in her. Now she extends the same kind of trust to her teams to grow and empower them.

Being open and transparent is a key part of trust. Tell your team your expectations and how to meet them. Then give them the space they need to get there and step away from micromanaging.

If you want your team to travel to Bluffton, South Carolina, from San Jose, California, there are several ways to accomplish this. Some routes take more time than others. Some are more or less expensive than others. Tell the team their destination, give them the parameters within which they can work (time, resources, budget, etc.), and then let them decide the best path to achieve the goal.

Without trust, you cannot begin to build the bridge.

HOW TO BUILD TRUST AS A MANAGER:
- Act with integrity
  - Be in alignment with what you say you will do

- Communicate with transparency
  - Set goals that are achievable and provide context around why goals and projects are important

- Give space
  - Once you communicate the goals, give your employee space to execute the goals

HOW TO BUILD TRUST AS AN EMPLOYEE:
- Perform with consistency
    - Trust develops through reliability and dependability on an ongoing basis

- Communicate with transparency
    - Inform your manager of any challenges or roadblocks so they are not surprised

- Ask questions
    - Clarify and ask for assistance as needed

CHAPTER 3:

Pillars of Respect

"If you want to be a great leader, remember to treat all people with respect at all times. For one, because you never know when you'll need their help. And two, it's a sign you respect all people, which all great leaders do."

~SIMON SINEK

Lack of respect can wreck the bridge you are building.

While trust is a belief in the reliability, truth, ability, or strength of someone or something, respect is the admiration of the person's qualities: their character, abilities, or behavior. Respect manifests in how someone treats someone else.

Trust is crucial when building a bridge between manager and employee. However, people often focus solely on trust and lose sight of respect. Respect is equally important to allow you and your team to show up authentically and have a psychologically safe space.

According to research by Georgetown University's Tony Schwartz and Christine Porath and published in the *Harvard Business Review,* nearly twenty thousand employees worldwide ranked respect as the most important leadership behavior. The higher the level of respect, the more engaged the employees are.

Schwartz noted:

In a meta-analysis of 263 research studies across 192 companies, employers with the most engaged employees were 22 percent more profitable than those with the least engaged employees.

Building respect creates solid relationships and healthy teams that are more profitable. More engaged employees have lower turnover.

Schwartz splits respect into two different types: owed respect and earned respect.

Owed respect is accorded equally to all members of a work group or an organization. It meets the universal need to feel included. Civility and an atmosphere suggesting that every member of the group is inherently valuable signal owed respect.

Earned respect recognizes individual employees who display valued qualities or behaviors. It distinguishes employees who have exceeded expectations and, particularly in knowledge work settings, affirms that each employee has unique strengths and talents.

In the workplace, an environment with too little owed respect often has micromanaging, abuse of power, and a feeling that employees are merely interchangeable resources. In contrast, when you see people taking credit for others' success or not recognizing employees' achievements, this is an environment with little or no earned respect among team members. Earned respect meets the need to be valued for doing good work.

Both types of respect are important. Too often, I have seen team members unnecessarily pitted against each other. Having earned respect does not mean one person is doing well and, therefore, others are failing. Instilling a sense of owed respect for all employees and managers creates a safe space for everyone to show up as they are.

It is important to note owed respect is not by position. Some managers inaccurately think they are *owed* respect because of a title. Owed respect is a universal human right. When someone with a title demonstrates skill, strengths, or talent, that is earned respect.

LACK OF OWED RESPECT BREAKS BRIDGES
Interestingly, of all the topics I discussed across the vast spectrum of people I interviewed—from CEOs to managers in a variety of industries—respect was the one topic where there were several stories about challenging bosses who did not respect their employees. Conversely, I found few stories about managers showing respect for their employees.

Vanessa had been at her company for four years and felt solid in her job. She had launched several products and felt like she was in a rhythm.

For the past year and a half, she had been working on a massive product launch. As the launch drew closer, her hours at work were ramping up while her hours for sleep were diminishing. She was completely exhausted. For the past few months, she had very little support. This was the biggest launch she had handled, and it was incredibly important for the company.

She was working so hard on this launch and became so exhausted she began coming to work in her pajamas in the morning. Her email inbox overflowed with yet more emails coming in one after another, and more work piled on. People stopped by her desk, requested changes, and asked for status updates.

One morning, she hit her breaking point. Sitting at her desk in her pajamas, she started falling apart from the crush of it all. Tears flowed down her face, the way they do when you do not mean for it to happen, but the frustration spills out as tears.

She had been crying for a little while when her manager, Brenda, strode over and snapped at her loudly.

"You need to pull it together. Leave your desk if you need to. You should not be crying here."

Don't you even want to know why I am crying? Vanessa thought.

"Pull it together," Brenda said curtly.

Then, without a word, Vanessa rose and walked over to a quiet area of the building where she could be alone.

She let it all go. She felt all of the overwhelm and exhaustion.

She was in shock.

First, she was in shock she was crying at work.

This isn't really in my control. I just hit a wall, she thought.

Second, she was in shock at how her boss was treating her. No empathy. No interest in knowing what was going on. There was no respect for what she had been doing. In this case, the owed respect is the respect for her as a human and not just as a resource.

As Vanessa started to pull herself together and then tackled the rest of her endless launch activities, she thought,

If I ever walked up to someone crying at their desk, I would invite them to a room to talk. Or I would ask if they want to go for a walk to see what is going on. I would tell them they could have the afternoon off and offer to cover for them.

Instead, a few things happened to Vanessa that day.

Vanessa lost respect for her boss, Brenda. Through Brenda's actions, Vanessa learned she needed to be robotic at work. She could not show emotion. She built up walls.

Unfortunately, this lack of owed respect was not an isolated incident. Brenda frequently shushed Vanessa in conversations. Brenda would have Vanessa send Vanessa's bullet points to present, and then Brenda would present them as her own.

Because of these actions and lack of respect, Vanessa, who was incredible at her job, lost a lot of her joy while working with Brenda. She also did not show up authentically. Brenda showed her it was not a safe space to express emotions or her opinions.

Luckily, Vanessa remembered the importance of respect when she began to lead teams. For many years, Vanessa has led teams and now leads marketing at a start-up. She gets to know the individuals on her team. When there is a deadline or a crunch time, she checks in.

"How are you doing with constructing the new presentation? What challenges are you encountering?" Vanessa asks.

"It is going well. I'm stuck on how to do some of the transitions, though," responded Amanda, her employee at the new start-up.

"Okay, let's go over the transitions and figure them out."

Vanessa not only checks in on how the team is doing with their project, but she also checks in to understand how each person is doing as a whole person. She thinks of her team not as a resource to finish a task but as humans. She respects their needs, abilities, and opinions—even if they differ from hers. She shows them owed respect. Because of this respect, she has loyal teams with low turnover and high engagement.

Respect is as important as trust, and, like trust, one must reinforce it with everyday interactions.

LACK OF EARNED RESPECT: COLLABORATION NOT COMPETITION

Several times during my interviews, I heard stories about managers who pit people against each other.

Pitting people against each other is an example of a lack of earned respect. This can be as detrimental as not having owed respect.

Vanessa, from the story above, had an experience with a lack of earned respect as well. When recruited to her current start-up, the CEO told her she would be solely in charge of the marketing team, which she is. However, the company was interviewing someone else, Lina, for another role and communicating to Lina she would be in charge of marketing, in addition to her other role.

When Vanessa and Lina started at the company on the same day and met each other, each one talked about running marketing as a part of her role. It was an awkward conversation, to say the least. The CEO eventually had to clarify the roles, which created a challenging place for them both. Again, Vanessa lost respect for her manager, the CEO. The two weeks of two people trying to do the same work were counterproductive and led to resentment between the two caused by the CEO.

I've had it happen to me as well. A past manager told me I would be in charge of defining a brand-new project. I worked on it for weeks and then found out he had told the same thing to someone else. I understand why you would have two people work on the same thing. Potentially, you are looking for lots of ideas. The challenging part is the competition against each other and the lack of transparency. Both of us lost respect for our manager.

When you are not open about what you are doing, it demonstrates a lack of respect for the people on your team.

PSYCHOLOGICAL SAFETY: COME AS YOU ARE
According to a 2021 McKinsey study, psychological safety is the belief you can voice ideas, questions, concerns, or mistakes without the risk of punishment or humiliation. It also creates a space where you can show up as your authentic self. McKinsey talks about the importance of creating a safe environment when building healthy, high-performing teams, and safety is important to include in the employee-manager relationship as well.

Being able to ask questions and offer ideas without fear of being judged or demeaned creates this openness. It allows for more free-flowing thoughts and innovations. The McKinsey study also notes that quite often, both sides (managers and employees) can be quick to say, "We can't do that," for the following reasons:

- It was already tried and failed.
- It is not something we support here.
- We don't have enough resources.

Similar to building respect through openness and transparency, another key is to stay curious.

Enabling people (managers and employees alike) to show up as they are can be freeing. We spend most of our life at work. Allowing people to show up as they are includes creating space for emotions and challenging times.

~ ~ ~ ~

Paul has been leading teams for over two decades. The thoughts in the forefront of his mind for all things:

- *What kind of team do you want to run?*
- *What do you want the experience of the people underneath you to be?*
- *How long do you want your people to stick around?*

As a tenured manager of program managers at a Fortune 500 tech company, he leads with respect. He is so well-known for his management style that three people had requested to be transferred into his group the week I interviewed him.

Paul works to have his team have the best experience possible. He views his one-on-one meetings differently than others I have talked to. He doesn't want an update in the meeting, as the teams cover those weekly.

Come to me with whatever else you have on your plate. It should not just be a status. ==Where is the challenge? How do you want to grow?== *Whatever else. You can come to talk to me about whatever. This is literally time for you.*

Sandra took this advice to heart, especially during the pandemic.

A few years ago, her father, Roy, who lived near Santa Rosa, California, had his house destroyed in a fire. She needed to go care for him to ensure he was moved in and settled somewhere new that could provide what he needed, as he had dementia. When she brought this up to Paul during their one-on-one, she was happy to hear his positive response.

"Of course. Go take care of him, Sandra. If you need to work half days for a while, no problem. I will comp you the time," he said.

Comping her time meant they would pay her for those hours, even though she was not working. Paul knew Sandra worked hard, and he respected her hard work. Recognizing her contributions and her needs as a human built the brick of respect between them.

Because of this, Sandra felt comfortable sharing with Paul when her father passed away. This was an incredibly challenging time for her, as it was a few months into the pandemic in 2020, and everything was under lockdown. She could not go out with her friends and talk to them. She used these status meetings with Paul to talk about her dad, what he was like, and how he was with her and her mom. Being an only child, not only did all of the responsibilities for taking care of her dad fall to her, but there was no one else she felt she could talk to about Roy and her memories. Paul would sit and listen to her stories of growing up with Roy and their family.

Because Paul has this policy of "Your one-on-one is your time. Use it as you like," he has built incredibly strong and resilient relationships with his team. He genuinely cared for Sandra. This care and respect create a bond and a bridge between the two. These hours and conversations reinforced that the respect and care were genuine.

Respect is not a checkbox inventory list in your manager or employee toolkit. In fact, showing respect is the opposite. A checkbox approach shows disrespect for someone, their feelings, and who they are as a person. Respect, as Paul demonstrated, needs to be genuinely valuing the whole person. This is true whether you are a manager or an employee.

MODELING EARNED RESPECT: SHE HAS IT
Melanie was an outside sales rep at a manufacturer's representative firm. After having corporate success working in high-tech/electronic components distribution (Fortune 500 companies), she took this prestigious position as a salesperson directly representing the factories.

One of the manufacturing companies they worked with was Mitsubishi Electronics. Wanting to excel in her position, Melanie always felt the need to find out more about the technical aspects of electrical engineering, which wasn't her background, so she could speak to the design in product and support the engineers with whom she worked.

Her manager, Sam, was about her age, open-minded, supportive, and with high emotional intelligence. He was also the owner's son.

Melanie and Sam had a great relationship. Sam greatly respected Melanie's ability and was a champion of hers. In fact, he was responsible for Melanie getting the position. He would often push her to do more when she held back or tried to overdo in ways that were not serving her.

During their one-on-ones, when he asked how things were going, she would talk about how she wanted to know more about the technical aspect ratios and specifications of the components.

"You don't have to know how fast they are, how much this heat sink dissipates, or how fast a semiconductor runs. You don't have to know every single in and out. We're not expecting your position to be that technical."

Melanie, as many of us would have, sighed with relief upon hearing his expectations.

"This is about you helping to solve the problems. We want you to know how to find solutions and be able to communicate with the engineers, not do their jobs for them."

Melanie was the first female sales rep in this firm. At that time, there were not a lot of female outside sales reps, especially working with a semiconductor manufacturing company. Often the other more senior reps would be a bit reticent about having her on the account. Sometimes they were even disrespectful, skipping over her in meetings or referring to a male counterpart not involved with that client. Not Sam.

Melanie worked hard and had proven herself. Through his actions and words, Sam showed the earned respect he had for Melanie.

"Melanie has this. This client loves her. Mel, why don't you go through where they are in the cycle, what the development timeframe looks like, and what support they need."

By Sam noting this about Melanie, he was highlighting the earned respect he had for her, thereby signaling that others should respect her and her skills and abilities as well. With this act of Sam having her back, the others began to respect her more and more. Ultimately, Melanie excelled in this position.

As a manager, it is important not only to tell someone you trust in their ability to deliver and respect them but also to show your level of respect to others. Being consistent in what you say one on one with what you say and do in front of others also builds respect as well as trust.

INVESTING TIME TO DEVELOP YOUR EMPLOYEES ENGENDERS INCREASED RESPECT

When I knew Derek a number of years ago, he was the head of a division at a consumer-packaged goods company. He was always smiling and had such an infectious laugh you could hear through the walls that would make others smile.

I always felt my opinions mattered to him, even though I was a few levels lower than Derek when we worked together. One afternoon, after presenting some research findings on a well-known barbecue sauce to Derek and his leadership team, he pulled me aside privately to provide guidance on how to frame up the recommendations differently the next time I delivered results. I respected him so much for giving me the advice.

Derek had a similar experience with Rich, the General Manager of Derek's division. They had just finished a negotiation with a massive brand. It had taken several weeks to get all the details ironed out and aligned. After finalizing the deal and dotting all the i's and crossing all the t's, Rich brought Derek into his office.

"Great job with the negotiation, Derek. What did you learn?" Rich asked.

This was the first time Derek had negotiated a deal in this way. Rich wanted him to reflect on what went well and what did not so he would retain the learning for the next negotiation Derek was involved with.

Several months later, Derek presented Rich with a full plan for his products.

"Derek, this is the perfect plan for a business we want to sell," said Rich.

"But this is very in line with what the business has been delivering over the past couple of years," Derek said.

"Yes, but this is a nonstrategic business for us. Nonstrategic businesses have to outperform the company either on sales growth or profit growth. A nonstrategic business isn't serving its role in the company if it is simply growing at the company average rate, even if the average is good."

By investing the time in Derek to grow him, Rich earned Derek's respect—the same way Derek earned my respect. Derek and Rich modeled how important it is to think through situations instead of simply how to execute in a given situation.

~ ~ ~ ~

Focusing on building the brick of respect will pay massive dividends for you. Understanding the environment of your company will inform which type of respect you should lean into in which situation. Creating a relationship with high respect will have a ripple effect on the rest of the team.

Respect ranks as the most important leadership behavior, which means this ripple effect can change the health and happiness of the full team.

HOW TO BUILD RESPECT AS A MANAGER:
- Start from the beginning with owed respect. Treat all employees with equal respect, as any human is deserving of.
- Lift people up. Avoid pitting them against each other. This only hurts the team, and others see what you are doing.
- Leverage individuals' talents. You have diverse people working for you. Understand and respect the abilities, ideas, and opinions they bring to the table.
- Foster collaboration. If there is competition, make it about the goal and not a competition against the other person with subterfuge.
- Create space for them to bring their whole selves to work. Check in and see how they are doing.

HOW TO BUILD RESPECT AS AN EMPLOYEE:
- As with the manager, begin with owed respect. How would you want it to be if you were the manager?
- Notice how you speak about your manager to others. Wherever you work, even if it is in a fully virtual environment, word can easily get around.
- Identify the aspects of your manager you respect and admire and cultivate those parts of the relationship.

Both respect and trust are important parts of the bridge. Creating a connection between manager and employee is the brick that completes the foundational pieces necessary for a sturdy bridge.

CHAPTER 4:

Creating Connection

"Connection is why we're here. It is what gives purpose and meaning to our lives."

~BRENÉ BROWN

I can still smell the freshly cut lumber and hear the buzz of the saws when I think of my grandfather, Gordon Wilson, who was the general manager of the Hines Lumber Mill. With his solid 6' 3" frame and Levis, he looked every bit the part. One cool summer day, as we strode through the mill, my small eight-year-old hand slipped inside his.

My grandfather would stop and chat with every operator in the mill individually. I remember being struck by his demeanor. I was amazed he knew each by name as well as their spouses and children.

"Hi, Cal, how is school going for Mary? Is she enjoying third grade?" Gordon asked.

"Things are going well, Mr. Wilson. She really likes math this year," Cal said.

We continued our tour through the mill.

"How long does Raul need to be in the cast? Is it still just a few more weeks?" Gordon asked Micah.

"We go to the doctor to check at the end of the week," Micah said.

"Well, tell Andrea our thoughts are with all of you. We want Raul to have a quick recovery so he can go play ball again."

With each of these small interactions, he was building a connection with his employees individually. Gordon Wilson was an honest, forthright man who always kept his word. He already had their trust and respect. It was important to him to demonstrate his respect and trust in them.

This walk he did each morning continued to build that bridge between him and his employees, strengthening their connection.

Connection is the art, or state, of being linked or creating a relationship between two people. In this book, we are looking at connection as creating a positive relationship at work between two or more people.

At the age of eight, I didn't have the words to name what my grandfather was doing, but even then, I could feel the positive impact he had on his employees.

I now know in creating this conncction, my grandfather had built strong bonds with all of his workers. They would go above and beyond to make the mill successful. In fact, financially, the mill was in the red when my grandfather began as general manager. Two years later, the mill turned a profit.

MASTER THE ART OF SAYING HI AND GETTING TO KNOW OTHERS

==Ask questions and find commonalities.== Where did they go to college is a common question. A friend, Jenny, told me about a woman who gave the corporate new hire trainings at a well-known brewing company in 2000. The trainer had two golden retrievers named Bonnie and Clyde. While Jenny does not remember her name, she does recall when this woman opened her laptop up to present and seeing the wallpaper with the cutest little fluffball puppies.

The new hire trainer had said, "These are my puppies. Show new work colleagues a little of you to break the ice and connect. It will go far."

Jenny has carried this advice with her.

A former colleague, Raymond, had an employee, Sera, who often complained about work. Raymond found it draining in their conversations and was looking for a way to connect more with her. He began asking her questions to get to know her more about her. It is important to note his interest was genuine. Finding out she liked dogs gave him the ability to connect with her and see her in a new light instead of as someone who mostly complained.

> *"What divides us pales in comparison to what unites us."*
>
> ~TED KENNEDY

When we find commonalities with others, we can see them in a positive light.

CONNECTION CAN BE BUILT (OR NOT) RIGHT FROM THE START

When Mai first began her job as head of marketing for a start-up, she was excited to jump in and make a big impact. While her laptop was waiting at her desk on her first day, there was no onboarding. Though she reported to the CEO, Rami, he did not even speak to her outside of meetings with the other executives during her first two weeks despite her request to have a one-on-one with him the first week she started.

"Good morning!" Mai cheerfully said when she passed Rami in the hallway.

He didn't acknowledge her and kept walking.

In the following weeks, the interactions Mai had with Rami were similar. He did not listen to her in meetings. He made little or no attempt to connect with her. This would foreshadow their interactions over the coming months. Rami supported her peers and dismissed her opinions and comments out of hand.

The lack of connection accompanied by his other actions led to Mai's lack of trust and respect for Rami. Instead of building a bridge, Rami was building a wall.

In talking to Mai about this experience, she compared him to Leslie, a former manager, who had been the complete opposite. Not only was everything ready for Mai when she started, but Leslie had also included a handwritten note on her desk. Her manager met with her that first day. Over the course of the first month, Mai and Leslie discussed growth opportunities in her current position.

"Where do you want to go? Where do you see yourself in one year? Three years?"

Leslie set the groundwork from the very start to build a connection with Mai, and Mai did the same thing with Leslie.

There is a well-known saying:

You never get a second chance to make a first impression.
~Unknown

As a manager, think about the culture you want to foster with your team. It continues with each person you bring on to your team.

As an employee, think about how you want to be viewed by your manager and as part of the team, which can begin as early as the interview process. A good friend told me about interviewing with a large tech company where her (future) manager connected with her, showing genuine compassion and interest in her. She told me at that moment she decided this was the company and manager she wanted to work for.

It is further cemented by your behavior each day with them, starting on your first day in the office or virtually. Work on creating that connection from day one. As an employee, come in with a smile and a great attitude. As a manager, help your employee feel welcome.

People are not just resources. They desire connection.

A December 2021 article in *Forbes Magazine*, "Why 2022 Is the Year of Workplace Culture," cited:

ADP Research Institute found that US workers who feel strongly connected to their employers are seventy-five times more likely to be engaged than those who do not feel connected.

Engaged employees are more likely to have a higher rate of retention. While lack of respect was a common theme for bridge destruction, it was also common to hear and read story after story about how connection drove not only the creation of the bridge but its maintenance as well as its repair.

PERSONALIZE HOW YOU LEAD YOUR TEAM

Connor had been at a large high-tech organization for nearly a decade. He was interviewing for his team and met with his manager, Linda, to discuss a recent interviewee, Max. Linda felt like something was off about the energy for the team and ended up passing on him. Later Max joined a team that Connor moved onto. Over the next year, Connor realized how effective Max was at his job. Though his energy and process were completely different from Connor's, Max's way was equally effective. Connor and Max became friends, and in an interesting twist, after Max moved off the team, he recommended Connor come to manage the team.

In thinking about this new team and Max, Connor thought:

This guy is very talented. He does things very differently than I do. I can't tell him to do things my way. It would not work for him. The same way that I could never do things the same way he does.

Connor understood Max had a different style, which he respected and did not seek to change.

I need to trust people to figure out what works for them.

Now Connor intentionally identifies the strengths and opportunity areas of his employees. He provides them with guidance and suggestions and then lets them get to work in a way that works for them as well as meeting the goals of the project. He noted this was the most important lesson he learned as a manager, as it yields huge dividends in terms of trust and respect among his teams.

~ ~ ~ ~

A CEO of a start-up, Penelope, has an employee, Lincoln, who is incredibly gifted at building communities and crafting stories. Several months in, Lincoln came in to chat with Penelope and shared something he did not share with most managers. Because they worked closely together and developed a strong connection, Lincoln felt safe confiding in Penelope.

"I have ADHD, which can sometimes be challenging for me," Penelope said.

Penelope and Lincoln worked together on how they could best communicate with each other and create the best environment for Lincoln to thrive.

Both of these stories illustrate how important it is to get to know your employees. Another component of this is what motivates them.

Another way to engage employees and managers is to understand what motivates them. Jennifer Britton, author of *Reconnecting Workspaces in the Hybrid World* and I spoke about this. She has a framework on motivation called CLAIMS, the seven ways people can be motivated. Based on our conversation and my research, I have added an extra "s" ("status") for both employees and managers to Britton's framework:

- Community
    - Some want an organization that creates a community they enjoy. This can be anything from a very diverse community to one that feels like a close-knit family.
    - As a manager, consider the type of community that will serve your team best. Do they like activities? Do you and they enjoy socializing?
    - As an employee, how can you add to the community? What extra *flavor* could you bring to add to the *soup*

of this community that is the team or the organization at large?

- Learning
    - Some are compelled by learning opportunities or ways they can grow and stretch.
    - What are those things for you as an employee or a manager? Ideas could be attending conferences, learning to code, or improving speaking skills.

- Autonomy
    - How autonomous do you want to be?
    - Some people thrive on little instruction, and others like to receive more explicit directions. Where do you fit?

- Impact
    - This is about understanding the connective tissue to what you are doing and what the company is doing. What impact are you having here?
    - This could include influencing team or organization goals in observable ways that connect their work to mission success.

- Monetary
    - Some are driven by salary. They may have external goals they want to attain (house, car, college) that their salary enables. (Note: This is extrinsic and can be temporary.)

- Service
    - Some have a strong desire to give back. Companies offer benefits aligned with this, like extra paid time

off (PTO) hours to build houses or work in a soup kitchen.
- When I have volunteered as a part of a group, it has always improved the bond we have as a team.

- Status
    - For some, a title is important. They are looking for the next promotion. Understanding that and helping them (as an employee for your manager or as a manager for your employee) can make you a rock star.
    - This can also be a role where they are a subject matter expert or a mentor to others.

More options exist than salary (and stock options). Some people like public recognition (occasional recognition that is a bigger deal) while others like private recognition and more frequently. Some want to move up to the next title, and others want to stay where they are. Some want to know the impact they contribute. Knowing what motivates your employees can help you craft the best ways to keep them motivated and engaged.

As an employee, it is important to understand what motivates you and communicate this to your manager. Again, we are building the bridge from both sides.

We can move beyond motivation to inspiration. Connect with why you and your team are excited about the work and the organization. How does that purpose tie to what you are doing? When I worked on a team trying to accomplish something I was passionate about, I enthusiastically dove into the project. The link to purpose can be the impact you are making. Understanding this purpose and passion of you and your team transforms motivation into inspiration.

~ ~ ~ ~

Tamara Sniffen, Vice President of Commercial Excellence and Biologics at Stryker, a medical equipment manufacturing company, wanted to express her gratitude for her top leaders and their first quarter (Q1) performance. Knowing some of them like to entertain, she found gorgeous cards with ideas to create easy, fun, and absolutely delicious charcuterie boards for every occasion—from an everyday dinner party to dessert platters to a festive Easter brunch. With each one, she included a tailored handwritten note to each leader thanking them for the specific things they did that quarter.

In this time when we receive so much *junk mail*, how nice is it to receive a personal gift with a handwritten note? Tamara knows her team and knows how much this gesture means to them. Even though she is incredibly busy, she takes the time to personally reach out and send them something meaningful.

WHAT'S YOUR STYLE?

While there are the classic communication styles (assertive, aggressive, passive-aggressive, and passive), Mark Murphy and his team at Leadership IQ created another set of four communication styles after years of research. A *Fast Company* article in 2019 details Murphy's four communication styles:

- Analytical: Think data.
- Intuitive: Think big picture.

- Functional: Think process.
- Personal: Think emotions.

The *analytical style* prefers concrete figures and direct conversations. Often, the conversation is mostly logical and without much emotion. One tip is to avoid sentences that begin with "I think..." or "I feel that ..." Ambiguous or cryptic language can be annoying for this type. They want to make decisions with facts.

In contrast, the *intuitive style* is a big-picture thinker. Data, facts, and figures are not the way to converse with this style. Instead, paint the picture with a broad overview. Focus on the results and not the process. Don't jump into the details with this type. However, you'll want to be able to answer any follow-up questions they may have. This type is efficient and always on the go, getting things done. Going through something step by step can be exhausting for this type. Keep the topic focused on the big picture, and this type will ask for details as needed.

The *functional style* prefers process. Step by step, with an ordered logic to the process, is helpful for communicating well. I imagine this type as a program manager with a timeline. In working with this type, you want to have active listening (See Actively Listening chapter) and ask follow-up questions to confirm what they have said and ensure you are both on the same page. This type is very thorough. When communicating with them, you may want to guide the conversation and ask specific questions.

With the *personal style*, they lean more toward relationships. They love to connect with people. They are great listeners and truly care about what the other person is saying. They can bring the team together. Starting conversations with a check-in about how things are going before jumping straight into business is important for this style. Conversations are a way to get to know others and not just about business.

Whether you are an employee or a manager, knowing your own communication style is helpful for you and for the others who want to communicate with you. The same is true for you knowing others' communication styles to communicate effectively with them. Communicating in a way that works well for your manager or employee can help ensure you are both heard and aligned.

~ ~ ~ ~

As discussed in the How We Got Here chapter, a 2022 Gallup article "US Employee Engagement Drops for First Year in a Decade" found that two of the three main drivers of the 2021 decline in employee engagement were clarity of expectations and being able to do your best work. Better communication of expectations and what you want your employee to do (and enabling that) can lead to better employee engagement, which is better for the organization.

Also consider the preferred mode of communication. As a manager, does your team prefer email, text, or instant messaging on Slack or Teams, etc.? What is your preferred mode? Have you discussed this with your team or your manager? As an employee, what is your preferred communication?

All of the great managers I spoke with had a common thread—knowing their team as well as customizing their style to meet those they are managing because management is not *one size fits all*. It is *one size fits you*. (Note: You refers to the employee.) Effective leaders customize their style to meet the needs of each of their employees on the team.

I had an employee who was her happiest when we would meet for five minutes at the start of each day to discuss her objectives and then spend five or ten minutes at the end of each day reviewing her progress. For me, this would have felt like micromanaging and a lack of trust from my manager. For her, she felt a sense of direction and accomplishment. She told me this gave her a solid sense that we were on the same page, partnering together to accomplish everything. These ten or fifteen minutes of my day were well spent. She was always happier, more effective, and able to finish more projects when we spent this time together.

According to a March 2020 *Harvard Business Review* article, 75 percent of employees say they feel more socially isolated. As a manager, if you build a connection with your team, you can help them feel less like an island on their own and more like they belong to the team. As an employee, you can also leverage the ideas given previously to build a connection with your coworkers as well as with your manager. Building that connection with ideas from above will help them be more engaged at work.

A MANAGER'S GUIDE ON THE MANAGER

Shortly after he started at a large tech company in Silicon Valley, Leon met with his manager, Stan, on a bench outside.

Leon was working as part of the retail marketing team on one of the product lines. It was their second one-on-one meeting.

"I'd like to walk you through a short presentation about my style, Leon," Stan said.

With that, Stan opened up his laptop and walked Leon through some slides that talked about Stan's leadership style. They discussed his management philosophy.

"I'm a bit of an extrovert and think my thoughts aloud as I work through them, Leon. These slides are like a cheat sheet for who I am as a manager," Stan continued.

It was all very upfront and laid out exactly who he was.

"My leadership style is more Socratic. I like to ask questions and have people come to their own conclusions instead of giving them the answer."

Stan told Leon he liked to have feedback. The approach was very bottoms up instead of top-down, where a manager simply tells you what to do. Leon could tell Stan was being very authentic and open about his style.

A couple of weeks later, Stan asked Leon in person during their one-on-one:

How can I support you? What can I do better? What feedback do you have for me?

Then he waited patiently for Leon to answer. He took notes of what Leon said and always followed up on it. He reinforced that by asking for feedback each week.

This enabled two things for Leon. First, Leon knew he could always go to Stan with feedback, and he felt empowered to say what was on his mind. He could address hard topics with Stan because he was so open to hearing what was on Leon's mind.

Second, he understood Stan's management style. Leon understood how to present to him and appreciated Stan's open-door policy, which meant Stan was fine with the *drive-by* instead of scheduled, preplanned discussions. When they faced a challenge on a project, Leon felt comfortable going to Stan and talking to him early on. Leon would go in with a solution and discuss it with Stan.

Because Stan modeled transparency and openness to feedback, Leon now leads his teams this way. Leon asks for feedback during his one-on-ones.

What can I do better? What could I help you with?

Leon found that one of his direct reports had errantly been left off an email chain from the CEO about a product initiative. She was very frustrated as she had worked on the project for months. Sonya went directly to Leon and let him know how she felt. He immediately added her to the thread. Leon chatted with Sonya about it and told her that he appreciated that she came to him directly.

Not every manager provides a slide presentation of their management style, as Stan does. As part of understanding your manager, find out how they like to communicate.

- How do they process information?
- Do they like planned meetings or casual drop-in meetings?
- How do they want to receive updates: email, Slack, text?

I had a manager who rarely read email. Her unread email inbox was over eight thousand. If you sent her an email, it was like putting it into an abyss. When asked about how she liked to communicate, she told me she preferred Slack. She was on Slack all the time and was much more responsive there.

Find out how your manager is motivated. Understand what their goals are. Look for ways you can help them achieve their goals. If you do not know this, set up a meeting and ask them about it.

FOSTERING CONNECTION WITH A COFFEE KLATCH

The pandemic has been challenging. With so many working from home, it has become harder to do a *drive-by* chat or a hallway conversation to create a connection. We have tried virtual games, virtual cocktail hours, virtual scavenger hunts, and virtual cooking classes. Everything.

To create a strong connection with your team, understand them in the ways discussed above. Here is a story of how it worked to connect a team and create a close-knit bond.

Peter, Software Group Director, leads regular stand-up status meetings. Everyone participates in those weekly. During the pandemic, they added one extra shorter (thirty-minute) meeting. Peter told them there would be only one agenda item or rule.

You don't talk about work. Anything else is fair game.

Peter's team talked about what was going on with their children or the challenges they were having. They talked about a great new recipe. There was a *lot* of recipe swapping. They discussed celebrating their children's birthdays and offered creative ideas. With these short weekly conversations full of chatter and invariably a lot of laughter, they built friendships and connections with each other and with Peter.

Peter also paid attention to those not commenting as much and invited them into the conversation through questions.

"Hey, Priyanka, how is your daughter doing? How does she like school these days? How is soccer going?" he asked.

He actively included everyone in the conversation. While this meeting was optional, it became a meeting everyone attended because, as they told Peter, the coffee klatch gave them a sense of inclusion and community—and a great way to have a break in the middle of the workweek.

As of April 2022, when this team was going back into the office part time, the team unanimously decided they wanted these meetings to continue. Interestingly, they voted to have it occur on a day when they were not in the office in order to bring them together when they were physically apart.

Building a connection does not always have to be one-on-one. Building connections can happen in a variety of ways. I have offered some ideas. Play with them and determine which ones suit you best.

My dad has often said, "Each person has a gift. It is there for you to find it."

Spend the time to find the gift with your employee or your manager.

With each part of building connection, it truly is that *one size fits you*—not a one size fits all style of managing or connecting. Understand what works best for you as an employee and as a manager.

HOW TO BUILD CONNECTION AS A MANAGER:
- Know your team to create the best personalized leadership style for you and your employees.
- Be authentic and provide recognition of how they prefer it.
- Ask your team questions about themselves. Get to know them, their families, aspirations, and motivations. Make it a game to find a new fact about them once a month.

> **HOW TO BUILD CONNECTION AS AN EMPLOYEE:**
> - Help your manager look like a rock star
>   - Knowing your manager will help you highlight them
>   - Provide them with sound bites to send up to their management about your performance
>
> - Be succinct with enough detail that they don't come back to you with lots of questions

For both managers and employees, be genuine with this. I had a manager who received some feedback or coaching to be more approachable and friendly. Everything she asked sounded like she was reading off a checklist. She did not make any eye contact. The attempt at connection felt forced and inauthentic to my colleagues and me.

Your manager or employee will know if you are not being authentic in your desire to connect or if your actions feel like you are doing so to curry favor.

With trust, respect, and connection, you have a solid foundation. Next, we'll focus on maintaining and reinforcing the bridge. It is important to remember that while trust, respect, and connection are foundational, they always need to be reinforced as well.

PART 2:

STRENGTHEN FOR HEALTHY RELATIONSHIPS

As a matter of course, every day, a bridge is decaying bit by bit. You need to reinforce it consistently with small interactions. Once you have a solid foundation of trust, respect, and connection, you can create a more solid foundation with more bricks that will strengthen the bridge.

The next three bricks are: *setting expectations and boundaries*, *gaining alignment*, and *belief and development* through *growth mindset*. By working on these, the bridge will be a smoother two-way path that both manager and employee will feel confident walking across. As with the foundation, the key is that these actions are intentional and consistent.

SET EXPECTATIONS AND BOUNDARIES

With high burnout rates and no separation of work and personal life, it is imperative to set expectations and boundaries upon which both sides agree. We consider response time, accessibility, and other factors in creating expectations and boundaries. Having these in place helps keep the relationships between managers and employers healthy and sustainable.

GAIN ALIGNMENT

Sometimes teams drive to different destinations due to a lack of alignment between manager and employee. When managers and employees are on the same page, driving the same priorities, projects, and vision, everyone is more engaged, and we can move mountains.

EXHIBIT BELIEF AND DEVELOPMENT
To create the strongest manager-employee bridges, once the foundational bricks are solidly in place, have a belief in your manager or employee and then act on that belief. For managers, this means creating opportunities for your employees to shine and giving them the breadth to do just that. In doing so, you are reaffirming your trust and respect in them as well as deepening the connection. For employees, it can be raising your hand and saying you want the opportunity or running with an opportunity and delivering exceptionally on it.

You do not necessarily need to read these chapters in this order. That said, establishing the foundation (see the prior section) is a prerequisite in the relationship before you can work on the next three bricks.

Similar to the first three chapters, there are tips for the manager as well as tips for the employee at the end of these next chapters. I drew from my corporate background as well as experience coaching clients and teams, dozens of interviews, and research.

Jump into the next chapters to reinforce the bridge you are building! Brick by brick, you will create a solid relationship.

CHAPTER 5:

Set Expectations and Boundaries

"The boundary to what we accept is the boundary to our freedom."

~TARA BRACH

"This job will take everything that you offer. So, define what you are willing to give to the job," said Steve, a Senior Product Marketing Manager.

I will never forget these words. I had just finished my iPhone Product Marketing interview with Steve, and we were walking out of the building to the parking lot.

"Happy to answer any other questions that you have about anything, Kimberly," Steve said with a smile. He had this easy demeanor about him.

"There is one other thing. This feels like an incredible job and very demanding. You have two kids at home. How do you balance all of it?" I asked.

"Well, I don't always. Here is the thing. This job will take everything you offer. So, define what you are willing to give to the job. What do your lines look like?"

I had not really thought of it in those terms before. During the drive back to my house that afternoon, I thought about various parts of the interviews from that day, and those words rang in my head.

Even with his words of wisdom, boundaries were challenging for me.

My husband is great at setting and holding boundaries.

"An email, a text, a Slack message… it is an invitation to answer. It's like a knock at the door," according to my husband.

Sometimes, it is important to answer those invitations immediately. Sometimes, they do not need immediate attention.

It is key to know what your boundaries are. Without defining boundaries well earlier in my career meant that work easily crept in, and as Steve said, work would take as much as I would allow. It definitely did when I worked at Nestle, a start-up, and then at Apple. It was not until Logitech that I more clearly set boundaries. Having them more clearly set enabled me to have better work-life integration.

Many people, employees, and managers alike, struggle to learn this lesson.

BURNOUT AND BOUNDARIES

In the workplace, we sometimes do not consider which areas are the most important to define, especially with the ever-changing environment. There used to be clear lines between work and life. With cell phones and emails, the lines became blurry over time as people were then accessible twenty-four seven. With the pandemic, the lines were all but erased.

Many believe the manager will impose the boundaries, and the employee must agree. If the manager wants it to be so, employees must be available twenty-four seven. However, creating and being consistent with your boundaries for both sides increases respect and trust while still allowing for productivity and healthy teams.

Boundaries can be both physical and mental limits. Some examples of physical boundaries are time (when you are available for calls), the response time (for messages), deadlines, amount of work, turnaround time, etc. Mentally, it is also *turning off* work to be present for other parts of your life.

Burnout existed before the pandemic but not to the level we have seen in 2020, 2021, and 2022. It has increased since the pandemic began, and new research shows we continue to experience a high rate of burnout.

The American Psychological Association's 2021 Work and Well-Being Survey of 1,501 US adult workers had astounding findings:

- Seventy-nine percent of employees had experienced work-related stress in the month before the survey

- Nearly three in five employees reported negative impacts of work-related stress, including lack of interest, motivation, or energy (26 percent) and lack of effort at work (19 percent)

- Thirty-six percent reported cognitive weariness.

- Thirty-two percent reported emotional exhaustion.

- Forty-four percent reported physical fatigue—a 38 percent increase since 2019.

These numbers show the toll of working the longer hours detailed in the How We Got Here chapter. This burnout is affecting our health and well-being. An answer to this can be in setting expectations and boundaries, which for many people will involve looking at the workweek differently.

A NEW OPTION GAINING MOMENTUM: FOUR-DAY WORKWEEK

The idea of working *smarter, not harder*, has been around for quite a while. The Society of Human Resource Management (SHRM) reported that nearly 23 percent of companies in 2019 had adopted a four-day workweek.

In April 2022, thousands of employees embarked on a massive worldwide pilot launched by 4 Day Week Global, a nonprofit associated with the University of Oxford that helps companies execute and measure the impact of a four-day workweek, according to a 2021 *Forbes* article (Bartel, 2021).

Two types of four-day workweeks have emerged over the years. One involves the entire company shutting down all (or most) operations for seventy-two continuous hours (either Friday or Monday). The other is a flex four-day workweek, where the employees can choose which four days of the workweek to work. Some companies I know design this team by team.

"From a financial perspective, research indicates that moving to a four-day workweek can reduce overhead and other costs to businesses. Employees not only take fewer sick days but are generally more productive. Thus, productivity per employee rises," according to the same 2021 *Forbes* article, which cites the benefits of a four-day workweek.

The article also cited worker productivity and employee satisfaction benefits as well:

The Society for Human Resource Management reports that 60 percent of organizations that utilize a four-day workweek also experienced higher productivity and increased employee satisfaction. Companies that make the switch may find it makes for a better work-life balance, allowing team members to become more engaged and more efficiently use their time and company resources.

Creating a four-day workweek is not a compressed workweek, as Bartel, the *Forbes* author, points out. This will affect burnout and mental health. The idea is for this to enable better work-life integration.

Iceland has already proven these results. Between 2015 and 2019, Iceland conducted large-scale trials of twenty-five hundred workers, reducing the workweek to thirty-five or thirty-six hours without a reduction in pay. A joint project by Autonomy and the research organization, Association for Sustainability and Democracy, analyzed the results (Kelly, 2022).

A February 2022 *Forbes* article cited the results, which showed employees were more productive and happier with shortened workdays. Revenue did not decrease during the trials. Worker stress and burnout lessened. Given the incredible results, the study led to a significant change in Iceland. Nearly 90 percent of the working population now have reduced hours or other accommodations.

Part of the success of a four-day workweek is in establishing boundaries, especially with time.

If a four-day workweek is not possible in your situation, consider what time boundaries you need.

KEEPING TIME FOR YOU
Defining boundaries can be critical, especially when it comes to your time. How do you create your time boundaries at work? What parts are the most important to you?

Sometimes it's hard to know the pieces that are important to you until work encroaches upon them. Quite often, setting time boundaries is where we run into complications.

While working at a well-known consumer packaged goods (CPG) company, Pat loved her job in marketing. She always took great pride in doing her work exceedingly well.

In the middle of a cold, Midwest winter, a call from her VP, Doug, interrupted Pat's morning with her 105-pound dog. Wanting to be helpful and responsive, she answered these morning calls during her walks, trying to juggle the phone and keep ahold of her dog.

"Hello?" she answered, bracing her phone between her head and shoulder as she wrangled her dog back from the tree.

"I have a few things to run by you for a moment. I'm driving into work now."

"Oh, okay, I'm..." she started to explain before being interrupted.

"Right. It will only take a few moments."

He launched into a conversation about some new marketing tactics he wanted Pat to test out. The phone call lasted another twenty minutes, which made her morning walk challenging.

No longer a time to ease into the morning and reflect, her daily walk became an obstacle course of trying to remember the marketing tactics, when they were to be implemented, and in which upcoming campaigns while cajoling her five-year-old black lab into staying on the path and not running after the gray squirrel that had darted off in front of them.

Gradually, the calls happened more frequently. Soon they were not only in the morning but also in the evening. Her VP would want to run a random suggestion by her. Very rarely was it anything that was time sensitive. Often, her mind wandered to thoughts of accidentally hanging up on Doug and how much of an impact that would have on her career.

The more this happened, the more Pat began to feel frustrated and unhappy. Her mornings and evenings—a time she wanted for her personal life—were being invaded. This frustration began to bleed into other conversations she had with Doug.

She would also feel tired and rundown going into the office each day. Over time, she realized in an effort to be thoughtful and considerate to Doug she was not looking after the time she needed to reset and recharge, to get ready for the day, or recover from the day.

While this story occurred several years ago, it is so crucial for today.

In 2020 and 2021, makeshift *offices* set up in bedrooms, living rooms, and kitchens completely erased the blurry line that once existed between life and work. According to an August 2020 *Bloomberg* article, a study of 3.1 million people in over 21,000 companies by Harvard Business School and

New York University showed businesses added a staggering 48.5 minutes of meetings in 2020 each week, as if we had any extra time. Zoom fatigue became a thing many people suffered from after way too many meetings.

Companies have been trying to figure out how to help people not burn out but are not fundamentally changing the workload of their employees. That is absolutely the key to solving the problem—organizations need to change the workload. That said, there are things that you, as the manager or the employee, can do in setting expectations and defining your boundaries. The first step is to have a discussion about what the boundaries are.

One morning, Pat ended up stopping the calls with a simple tactic. She stopped picking up when Doug called if it was before 8 a.m. or after 5:30 p.m. She created a solid time boundary, a line in the sand. Pat talked with Doug about this and then did not deviate from it. Establishing these boundaries enabled her to feel more relaxed at home. She was also happier at work and more focused at work.

"Your boundaries became legendary," Doug said to her years later. "You were very strict about them. I respected that about you."

She would check any message he left. If it was a true emergency, she would take care of it immediately. It rarely ever was.

If you set the time boundary that work can reach you anytime, day or night, that will be how they regard you. It is so easy to try to give everything in an attempt to be helpful and get everything done. You need to decide what the time boundaries are that work best for you.

HOLD MY CALLS, TEXTS, SLACKS... AND OTHER INTERRUPTIONS

We've been so conditioned to respond immediately to a phone buzzing. You hear an alert, and there is an involuntary moment of excitement or stress, depending on what it is.

When it is your manager or another higher up pinging you incessantly, many people feel the urge to look immediately at the message and address it in the same moment, no matter what time of day or what else is happening. Your anxiety about what might be going wrong and how your response, or lack thereof, will appear to your superiors can feel all-encompassing and overwhelming, giving you the impulse to respond now.

Maybe that isn't the healthy response, though.

According to a Healthline 2020 article citing Yamalis Diaz, PhD, a clinical assistant professor in the department of child and adolescent psychiatry at NYU Grossman School of Medicine, numerous text messages can alert your flight or fight system (Mastroiani, 2020). She found it can "activate your stress system throughout the day" to have these alerts.

That means all the stimuli throughout the day of text messages from work, Slack messages, the dinging of your inbox each time a new email comes in, can add to the stress you feel. A potential boundary can be turning off notifications during certain hours to stay focused.

Marni had recently joined an incredible finance company with a great reputation with its employees. She was enjoying her new role and settling in well the first few months. Slowly, she noticed a troubling trend with her manager, Tina. Last minute, urgent requests to redo a presentation for her manager's manager, Jackie, were becoming the norm.

Nearing five o'clock one Thursday, her manager messaged.

"Hi. I know you're out the door to head home, but I really need you to tweak the presentation for Jackie. It shouldn't take too long. We have a meeting tomorrow at 11 a.m. So, I'd like to see it first thing. Drive safe."

Nothing more. Nothing about what she wanted it to include or what really needed to be tweaked.

"So, what would you like to have changed?" Marni texted back.

"I feel like it doesn't work the way that it is. Can you rearrange the introduction? Add in some data. Make it feel more substantial. I'd like it to be upleveled."

Marni knew she couldn't call as Tina was still in a meeting. She also knew she dashed off the text just before Marni would leave for the day. Sitting in traffic for the hourlong commute home gave Marni plenty of time to mull over the day's events. These last-minute texts were happening more regularly.

As soon as she walked through the door at home, she fired up her computer to work on "upleveling" the deck for the meeting the next morning. She spent hours poring through the data to find the best information to back up the recommendations.

Ping, ping, ping, ping, ping. It was the following Tuesday and the same incessant sound of the Slack messages at 4:55 p.m. as she was packing up her computer, papers, and water bottle to head home for the night. The noises signaled a constant barrage of last-minute stream of consciousness that needed to be taken care of before the next day.

Marni's stomach started to churn. The discomfort of her stomach highlighted the stress of the situation. Not only were the last-minute messages a regular occurrence, so was this feeling of nausea.

Do I look now or wait until I get home? These last-minute requests are stressing me out and making me sick, Marni thought.

As she drove home, she thought about all the requests:

We need a redo of the marketing funnel for tomorrow's meeting. Please make sure it has all of the latest numbers.

We are having a meeting tomorrow. We'll need to update Jackie on the email campaign.

Let's pull all of our learnings together from last quarter for tomorrow morning.

Last-minute work is common in many jobs. The challenge with this one, and with managers like this, is that the manager often:

- Does not value the time put into the extra work

- Does not provide great direction on where to go (in this case, it is because Tina often did not ask or did not understand the Jackie's needs)

- Delineate between what is *needed* and what is a true emergency

Often, they canceled the meetings that were going to happen the next day, which meant Marni needlessly worked many hours at night. She would spend hours nauseated and worried if she could finish the presentation in time or to the exacting standards of her manager (the same manager who didn't provide much direction). Then the next morning, they would cancel the meeting, or management would skip her presentation and "get to it another time." Rarely, if ever, did Tina thank Marni for the time and effort that went into these last-minute requests.

Marni's story reminded me of a time when I was chatting with an executive assistant, Isabella, at a company I worked at—a very fast-paced company that was hard-charging. A colleague, Luis, ran up, frantically telling Isabella about an emergency he was experiencing and how he desperately needed her help. Isabella could see the sweat on his brow due to his anxiety. He didn't even notice me. He had interrupted our conversation midstream, not noticing that either.

Clearly annoyed and without saying a word, she pointed to a small sign on the front of her cubicle:

Be advised: Lack of planning on your part... does not constitute an emergency on my part.

Isabella then nicely said she would look into Luis's issue a little bit later.

Not only was she clear on her boundaries, but she also had a sign up to show her boundaries to others.

Marni ultimately decided to prioritize work-life integration and set up boundaries with Tina, albeit without the humorous signage.

After numerous canceled meetings and her hard work not being used, Marni began to understand Tina's last-minute demands did not have to be something where she turned her entire evening upside down. She began to put her boundaries into place. She stopped answering Tina's messages after a certain point in the day.

In creating this boundary, Marni created her freedom. The freedom she felt was incredible. Marni no longer drove home with knots in her stomach, waiting on pins and needles for another message to come in. She could enjoy taking a walk with her dog in the morning without worry or anxiety. It was now a time for her. Marni filled her evenings with long soaks in the bathtub and glasses of her favorite red wine. She also maintained a solid relationship with Tina, who ended up promoting her a year later.

It is important to set and clarify the expectations you have.

Like Ivan Pavlov's infamous experiment, where he conditioned dogs to respond to a stimulus (bell ringing), we have been *trained* to respond to the alert of a new message (the stimulus). Maybe it is time to retrain. If the message alerts are causing stress and nausea, change the expectation.

What happens if you don't answer the text message at 6 p.m.? What if you open up time for you? You need time to recharge each day. Think about the small and big ways that you are setting expectations. Choose to set the ones that enable you to create the life you want.

WHAT YOU DO VERSUS WHAT YOU EXPECT

Randall worked at a Fortune 100 tech company. He'd been there for over a decade. So had his manager, Murali. She was easily the hardest working person he had ever met, putting in roughly eighty hours a week every week. Surprisingly, she did not feel it was critical for her team to put in the same hours as she did.

"This is my life. My career is my life. I choose to do this. This is not what I expect of you," she said to Randall.

And she meant it. Her words and actions followed that up.

When Murali came back to ask about the status of a project one Friday afternoon, he knew she just wanted an update.

"It's not quite ready for prime time just yet," Randall said.

"Great. When can we discuss it?"

"Let's go over it Monday."

There was no expectation you had to work through the weekend or be available twenty-four seven, including weekends. Randall appreciated that Murali understood he and the rest of the team could choose to define their boundaries with their weekends.

This is something he has carried through to his teams. He is clear about defining what turnaround time should be. He is also flexible with them, as needed. He thinks about the whole person, not just their work self. He talks to them about defining their boundaries.

He knows having time to decompress on the weekends is imperative. Taking time for vacation helps you recharge and come back reenergized. He watches the vacation hours of his team to make sure they are taking time off.

He even lightheartedly tells team members, "We're good. It's not like we can't get along without you. We're not curing an incurable disease here."

Randall reminds his team it isn't worth missing your child's birthday or those special moments. He makes sure he has dinner with his family. He does not miss his son's baseball games or birthday parties. He sets the example for his team. He also enforces his boundaries with his management as well.

The cost to your personal life and your relationships is not worth it. This is why it is so important to define the boundaries that are important to you. As a manager, this is important because it also improves retention. You have happier, more engaged employees.

HOW TO BUILD BOUNDARIES AS A MANAGER:
- Define what your expectations are for accessibility—both for you and for your employee—and what that means.
- Decide what your turnaround time will be. How quickly will you turn something around? How quickly do you want work turned around?
- Meet with your employee and have an open discussion about the bullet points above.

HOW TO BUILD BOUNDARIES AS AN EMPLOYEE:
- Define what you want your work-life integration to look like. When are the hours you work? Will you accept messages outside of those hours?
- Define what your turnaround time for deliverables will be. What expectations do you have for your manager?
- Determine what, if any, are the exceptions to these boundaries.
- Meet with your manager and have an open discussion about these things.

Be consistent with these boundaries. If you are inconsistent, it is hard to know if this is a true boundary or a flexible guideline that is not important to you.

After creating a solid foundation with trust, respect, and connection, we've further reinforced the bridge by discussing, defining, and implementing boundaries.

The next brick in the bridge is alignment, which is important as it will ensure you are both on the same page and creating a bridge that is solid. Without alignment, you could be moving in two different directions at two different speeds.

CHAPTER 6:

Gain Alignment

"Everyone talks about building a relationship with your customer. I think you build one with your employees first."

~ANGELA AHRENDTS
(SENIOR VICE PRESIDENT, APPLE)

If your car wheels are out of alignment, your steering wheel pulls one way or the other, which can cause your car to drift. You don't end up staying on course. To remedy this, you need to take your car to a mechanic to align the tires on your car.

The same is true with managers and employees. If one is out of alignment with the other, that one can pull away and start to do something different that is not congruent with the goals.

All too often, managers and employees think of themselves as islands. They don't need anyone else. Sometimes a manager will just say something should be done, without any context or explanation, and believe that should be good enough.

Some employees have thought they did not need to manage up or have alignment with their management, even if that management was the board of directors.

Alignment is one of the keys to getting things done successfully.

Alignment is when a manager and an employee have the same understanding about the goals and objectives. A narrow definition of this would just be for the business. The other piece of this, as we have been discussing throughout the book, is understanding that the motivations, goals, and values of managers and employees are also beneficial.

SOMETIMES THE EFFORT IS NOT WORTH THE AWARD
If you are not in sync with what your manager is proposing, speak up and take action.

Naomi had the opportunity to work on this when she was managing up with a challenging boss at a major retail company. Her manager, George, was the type who loved awards and trophies. He littered his office with what the team called a "look at me" wall of them.

One summer, the communications team had just begun working feverishly filling out forms, crossing t's and dotting i's in order to win an award that required a lot of work to apply for but had little ROI. The year before, they had jumped through all the hoops and won the award. It was a "nice to have" award George had put on his trophy wall in his office for all to see.

The next year, when he began requesting the work to have it done all over again, Naomi decided to intervene. All around her, colleagues were getting worked up about the amount of time this project would require. Additionally, the team already felt overwhelmed with a number of big projects and a couple of high-profile crises, so Naomi knew it would be even more of a stretch to take the time to apply this time around. She knew the team was at a breaking point. Naomi remained calm and went to talk to George.

"I heard we are going for the PR award again," Naomi said, peering around the corner into George's office.

"That's the plan. I'm looking forward to it," George replied.

"Hmm… it is quite the undertaking, George. The team already has a lot on their plates. How does this compare to other things currently on our plate?"

"Well, this is very important."

"Great. I understand. Can we get some extra resources to support this, then?" Naomi inquired.

"Well, no, we don't have extra staff we can pull in for this one, unfortunately," George responded.

"Can we get a contractor to help with the overflow of work this is going to cause?" she asked, brainstorming solutions.

"We don't have the funds in the budget to support that at this time, Naomi."

"Well, George, I understand this is important to you. If we don't have extra help, other projects are going to slip because of the time and attention this award application will take. We know the scope, as we did it last year. It is a big undertaking. Given the workload we have, you and I both know the team is already very stressed," Naomi explained.

She continued, "Winning this award did not have an appreciable impact on the business last year. Something is going to have to give if we do this. Which of our current projects that we need for the business should we let slip in priority for this?"

With Naomi's help, George begrudgingly realized they could not move forward with his goal of the award, which was an award Naomi knew he only really wanted to add to his résumé. By asking questions in this way, Naomi was able to help George conclude this was not the best use of the team's time. (Note: In not being originally aligned, Naomi and the team were losing respect for George. In pushing back on George in an appropriate way, Naomi earned more respect from him.)

It can be challenging to gain this alignment with your manager, as you may need to have difficult conversations to achieve this. Once you have a solid foundation of trust, respect, and connection, you should have a relationship with your manager where you can push for alignment when needed. Knowing the communication style of your manager, as we discussed earlier, is also very helpful with this.

CHOOSE HOW TO BEST ALIGN

In her next position, Naomi would quite often ask these questions to her team and her next manager:

- "Are we pushing ourselves for the sake of pushing ourselves? Or are we pushing ourselves for a real deadline?"

- "Do we need to go this fast? Or can we take a break and think about what needs to be done?"

- "Think about pacing and priorities. Can something on our plates give a bit? What can we push off until later or do at 70 or 80 percent versus 100 percent?"

In saying this to her team, they could stop and reflect on what was truly important.

This is an important brick in building the bridge. As a manager, you are showing your team that you respect them and their time and are not just needlessly adding work. Part of ensuring alignment is checking in at regular intervals to confirm that you're still on the same page, as understanding can diverge as projects move forward and teams evolve.

Naomi was willing to get in, roll up her sleeves, and help as needed. The lesson she learned from George, though unintentional on his part was very valuable and continues to serve her to this day. In building alignment, she is reinforcing the respect.

From my own management experiences and research, I know how beneficial alignment can be for the team.

When you are strapped for time and resources, fall back and ask the questions:

- What is important about this deadline?
- What are the competing priorities?
- Which ones will drive the business in the best way?
- As Manager: Who on my team is best suited for the roles and responsibilities?
- As Employee: Create a waterline chart showing what you have for your projects. Realistically, what can you meet? What can you not meet? Projects you can meet go above the waterline, and projects that you cannot move below the waterline.

Each time I walked through this waterline activity with my team, it was invaluable. For example, when the marketing team I was running had too much to tackle, we convened in a conference room to walk through the projects for the next quarter. We discussed the impact of each—plotting them into high, medium, and low—as well as the level of work required with a high, medium, and low scale to size them. We then ranked each of the projects and drew a line showing what we would be able to accomplish. By doing this process as the full team, I was able to understand the full team's capacity. As well, this enabled the team to have a say in what we would be working on and why.

The brick of alignment also reinforces parts of the foundational bricks along the way—trust, respect, and connection.

PEOPLE UNDERESTIMATE THE POWER OF ALIGNMENT
Alignment isn't something they teach you in business school when you are working toward your MBA, but it is a crucial skill that can literally make or break the success of a project—or your career at an organization.

Roger was a Senior Vice President working at a Fortune 500 company, and his task was to rebuild the team, reposition the brand, and create a product pipeline. Roger had been pulling in people he had previously worked with before, a strategy many employ in this situation. Full of ideas and excitement, he was tackling this head on.

The current products were languishing in the slowing market as the tech company had not kept up with the new trends. Within a few months, the new team was in place, brainstorming ideas to flesh out the new pipeline. Though he was excited about his ideas, he did not want to share them with others, as he was concerned another business unit would take the ideas and present them as their own. He chose not to share them with his management or any of the other business unit leaders.

In the spring, roughly eight months into Roger's position, he was set to present to the board, as all business units would do over the next two days. He was ready, he thought, walking to the conference room, the smell of strong coffee lingering in the air. He looked around to see the rest of the Executive Leadership Team and the Chairman of the Board, Vernon. His team followed him in and sat in the back right corner, smooshed into the packed room.

The air felt heavy. Maybe it was from the session before. Or maybe it was foreshadowing what was to come. Some of the faces of the business leaders around the table looked open and interested while others looked incredibly skeptical.

As Roger started to present, he tried to lighten the mood with some jokes. His jokes fell flat with his audience. He quickly moved on to talking about his analogy about finding the summit that the team could reach to bring the brand to the next level.

Even though they slotted the meeting for ninety minutes, the Executive Leadership Team and Vernon peppered Roger with questions for over two hours.

"You said we are learning to climb to the summit in this new world. How long will it take? Do you have the right people in place now?" asked the Chairman, Vernon, clearly skeptically.

Before Roger could respond, Vernon continued, "No matter. How are you going to market what you currently have?"

"Marie has that plan. Marie, why don't you talk about what we are going to do?" Roger interjected.

Roger turned abruptly to Marie, happy for the reprieve. Marie explained the marketing calendar.

"And the ROI? When will that be positive?" Vernon bellowed.

Roger was not prepared for that question or for several of the questions that followed. This was his third time presenting to this board. Previously, it had been relatively benign. This time, it was different. It was almost combative. Roger met the combative words in kind.

Over the next several months, though Roger didn't see it as it was happening, the belief, trust, and even respect the Executive Leadership Team had in him was diminishing. Each Board meeting became increasingly more challenging. The business was now in a precarious position already.

When he presented to the board in the fall, they skewered everything about the presentation.

"Where is the logic behind this plan?" asked one of the General Managers of another business line.

"How is there any credibility to this?" questioned another.

"This plan has numerous holes in it," concluded the Chairman, before the presentation of the plan was barely halfway through.

Other business plan presentations did not have the same reception that fall day. There was a big difference. The other general managers made a concerted effort to meet prior to the sessions and vet their plans with each other as well as with the rest of the Executive Leadership Team. They knew many of the concerns board members would raise. They either addressed them ahead of time and modified what they were proposing, or they were ready for the questions that would arise in the business planning session. Through these conversations, they gained the crucial alignment they would need for their programs to move forward.

Roger, on the other hand, was concerned that others would steal his plans, which was why he intentionally did not share them. With this mindset, it was challenging for Roger to see the possibilities of the yes/and approach to building his plans. He went into each board meeting a bit blind, without alignment, lacking connection and solid relationships with his peers. Without that, the leadership team had numerous questions and unraveled the plan.

The Executive Leadership Team would have backed him potentially if he had met with them and explained his plan. Instead, he presented it to everyone in the meeting at the same time. Just like dominoes falling, it was picked apart by one leader questioning one part of the plan, which led to another leader and then the head of a cross-functional department and then another.

He had no allies to back up his plan. There was no alignment on what he was proposing. No one would advocate on his behalf. It would have helped to have sent out the slides ahead of time, as requested by the Executive Leadership Team. This eroded the trust and belief his management had in him as well as the trust and belief those reporting to him had. That was the beginning of the end for him, and he didn't even know it.

Some of this is easy to see in retrospect.

THE PREFLIGHT MEETING AND HOW IT CAN SAVE YOU

I have always been a proponent of what I like to call the preflight meeting. It is a time when you gather the important stakeholders to understand their needs, wants, concerns, goals, and motivations, specifically around given projects. It is key to gaining alignment and is great for also building solid relationships and trust. In doing this, I know where things may go sideways before there is a more formal meeting. I also meet with stakeholders above me to do the same thing.

A great example of this came from when I worked at an organization that held quarterly prioritization meetings. A month before each quarter began, each business unit would present the marketing projects that they wanted to pursue to the heads of the various teams where they would need resources: design/UX, email marketing, online marketing, copy team, etc. Invariably, I proposed a bit over my share of projects, as I was on the new business side of a new product. Each time, the majority of my projects would move above the waterline, which meant my teams could move forward and pursue them.

Before meeting with my counterparts, I would speak with my manager to advocate for the projects I believed would be the most impactful, and we always aligned to the prioritization of projects and what scope we could adjust, if my counterparts pushed back on what they would be able to accomplish.

Here's what I did differently than some of my counterparts:

- I understood which key players and decision-makers would be in the room.

- I spoke with my cross-functional partners, highlighting the impact (both in quantitative sales units and in increased awareness—a number that we did not measure) that this project would have and why it was essential.

- I also outlined who we would need, for what duration of time, and if we could modify that with creative solutions. For example, sometimes we could use a contractor or outside vendor to make it faster or lessen the resource impact of someone internal that was in demand.

- After this conversation (one-on-one), I left them with a business case to speak to their management about.

- We did all of this well ahead of the quarterly prioritization meetings.

In meeting with my counterparts ahead of time, we were able to collaborate and design the ask that would be approved. They understood how important it was to the business in meaningful ways. I understood how much they could allocate resource-wise to the projects I was proposing. We would creatively devise a solution where we would all align. This allowed us to meet all of our objectives.

By providing a case (impact on the business; type of project; resources needed, i.e., time, money, people) and collaborating with my cross-functional partners, they were able to gain alignment more easily with their management. I gained a reputation for being the cross-functional lead that was creative in how we could achieve the goals on both sides. My product's websites were redesigned when others were not.

This also meant during the prioritization meetings, not only were my projects given the green light, but the pre sentations were also significantly shorter than anyone else's, as my cross-functional partners had already briefed their management. Everyone was already in alignment.

While these preflight meetings did not take much additional time, they saved massive amounts of time and headache for me that would have happened after the prioritization meetings (and did during my first quarter at this organization). If projects were not approved in the meeting, you had to have follow-up meetings to determine whether the projects could be approved for that quarter or not. It was a long process.

There are also some benefits not readily seen. Having this alignment made my counterparts look great for their management. I spoke highly of each of them and noted our collaboration, a top value this Fortune 500 company often touted. All of this combined to strengthen and reinforce the trust and respect my colleagues had for me and I with them.

In building alignment with my manager ahead of time, she enabled me to have free rein. The more I delivered (and overdelivered), the more that reinforced the trust. I always aligned my goals with my manager's goals. Had I acted as an island and only out for myself, none of this would have been possible.

HOW TO BUILD ALIGNMENT AS A MANAGER:
- Be clear on goals (SMART goals)
- Keep the goals interesting to your employee to increase engagement
- Explain how they fit into the bigger picture
- Check in regularly to confirm you're still on the same page (flying in the same direction)
- Understand your employees' motivations

HOW TO BUILD ALIGNMENT AS AN EMPLOYEE:
- Know your manager's goals
- Make sure that your goals align with theirs
- Help your manager shine with their manager
- Write out your highlights each week and send them to your manager
- Have preflight meetings with your boss (and key stakeholders)

Building alignment works well once you establish trust, respect, and connection (See prior chapters on how to establish). And in building alignment, you are not only strengthening the bridge, you are reinforcing the trust, respect, and connection you have with your employee or with your manager.

By defining boundaries and creating alignment, the bridge has become very solid. We will next look to the brick of belief, as having belief in your employee and your manager will further strengthen the bridge.

CHAPTER 7:

Exhibit Belief and Opportunities

"The way you see people is the way you treat them, and the way you treat them is what they become."

~JOHANN WOLFGANG VON GOETHE

What makes a flea stop jumping?

If you put a flea in a jar, it will jump out immediately. They know no limits. However, once a lid is on the jar, the flea continues to jump and hit the lid. Eventually, the flea stops jumping high enough to hit the lid.

In Stephen M.R. Covey's book, *Trust and Inspire*, he offers an example of how we, like the flea, can stop jumping.

The flea learns and becomes conditioned by its new reality. Interestingly, if you remove the lid, the flea will no longer jump out of the jar, according to the parable, even though the flea is still capable of doing so.

This same situation happens with a manager or an employee, conditioning and pigeonholing the other. Something happens and one side assumes the other person will remain that way. When a manager assumes the employee will always be a certain way, the limited potential the manager sees could lead to career stagnation for the employee or the manager may begin to micromanage, which can be the death of creativity. Empowering employees and teams leads to innovative results. The underpinning of both actions is the belief in what the person or team can become.

Without a leader even mentioning the words belief or trust, actions highlight how much a leader believes in the employee. If you are micromanaging your employee, it often means—or at the least implies—you do not believe they can complete the project.

On the other hand, empowering employees and providing them with opportunities shows the belief you have in them—the ability for them to be more than what they are at the moment. This belief, which goes hand in hand with a growth mindset, is one of the key ways to reinforce the bridge between an employee and a manager.

It can also work the other way around with the employee inferring something about the manager after a few interactions and then making an assumption that the manager will not change.

ADOPT A GROWTH MINDSET

Carol Dweck, Stanford University psychologist and renowned author, talks about the growth mindset and a fixed mindset in her book *Mindset, The New Psychology of Success*. She said:

In the fixed mindset, everything is about the outcome. If you fail—or if you're not the best—it's all been wasted. The growth mindset allows people to value what they're doing regardless of the outcome.

Dweck uses examples to show how people can change their behavior based upon what they end up thinking about someone else, as well as what they think someone thinks about them. She talks about how teachers treat students differently if the teacher the prior year provides feedback saying that the child is smart (or not). For example, Nate teaches fifth grade. If he tells Jason, a sixth-grade teacher, that Logan is smart, Jason will treat Logan as if he is smart. The opposite was also shown to be true.

Let's translate this example to business. If an employee makes a mistake or a manager does, which happens, as we are all human, the fixed mindset then decides that giving an opportunity to the person was a waste of time. A fixed mindset believes intellect and talent are finite. You are smart—or you are not. You possess certain skills and talents—or you do not. The fixed mindset does not believe in developing talents, intellect, or abilities. The fixed mindset asserts that if you make the mistake, you will continue to make the mistake. With a fixed mindset, you believe the other person cannot change, which then leads to reinforced negative assumptions.

With a growth mindset, on the other hand, the focus is on learning and the journey. If something goes *wrong*, you have the ability to learn and grow from it, knowing you have improved and not berating yourself for it. Time is not a waste when you learn from what is happening. Similarly, you believe others can learn, improve, and grow. Offering opportunities is a path to growth.

Successful inventors and entrepreneurs need a growth mindset. As an inventor, Edison made one thousand unsuccessful attempts before inventing the light bulb. If he had a fixed mindset, he would not have continued to try and iterate. The growth mindset asserts people can change and learn, which is just what Edison did with his inventions. People grow and become more than they were today or yesterday.

This is why belief is so important. As a manager, expect the best from your employee. As an employee, step into the next level of expectations.

A HOLIDAY OPPORTUNITY TO SHINE
Through my interviews and research, I have found that belief quite often needs to start with the manager.

CJ was very independent and had already led teams when he started his Leadership Development program at Home Depot. As part of this, he participated in a six-month management rotation at a local store. From the start, he thrived in the position. His manager, Ralph, was welcoming and put him in charge of the paint section as his first assignment. Ralph gave CJ broad ideas and let him go figure out what to do.

To get acclimated, CJ perused the paint section and chatted with his new coworkers. Before long, he was coming to his manager with numerous ideas about the paint section and how to change and improve things. With an open-door policy, his manager was always available by text, cell, or in person. In being accessible and listening openly, Ralph created an environment of trust from the very start between the two of them.

A few weeks in, CJ's manager pulled him aside to talk about a new project he wanted him to lead—a two-week sales competition to see which store in the region could sell the most paint as a holiday promotion.

"I want you to get into this competition. You come up with the ideas," Ralph told him. "Tell me what they're going to be, and we'll implement them. You can go ahead and run with this."

CJ was excited. This freedom lit up his creativity. After discussing the details of the competition, he left to meet with the other employees, eager to share ideas he already had. He brainstormed more ideas with them.

After working on it for a bit, CJ checked in with his manager.

"Run with your ideas. I trust you, CJ."

CJ and the team worked diligently to create and assemble an incredible paint display. It was a true labor of love, carrying in all the cans of paint. With gallons of beautiful Behr paint, CJ designed a holiday display to highlight numerous decorating ideas poised in the perfect position right in the front of the store near the cashiers.

At the end of the two weeks, the team was thrilled to find out they had won the district contest, and they were even more excited to find out they would move on to regionals. Belief from CJ's manager inspired creativity and helped the team win the regional and district holiday competitions.

Because Ralph created an environment where he believed CJ could live up to the task, CJ felt comfortable sharing ideas about how to improve things. Ralph then doubled down when he offered CJ the opportunity with the holiday paint competition. Offering that opportunity enabled CJ to show up with creativity and enthusiasm. This is where the belief can become a virtuous cycle. Once you build it, the employee steps up, as CJ did. This then instills more confidence for a manager to have more trust and offer more opportunities.

Before this experience, CJ thought it was important for a leader to provide lots of structure and details on how to do things. He realized in doing this that he was not believing in his team. CJ thrived in his management rotation program with a manager who allowed him to find his way and stretch his wings. This experience taught him how to give his employees more space, thereby empowering his teams. In doing that, he shows them he trusts them. From leading finance teams at Intuit to working in the Peace Corps, he has excelled throughout his career and always added in the brick of belief of what his team can do.

> *"It doesn't make sense to hire smart people and then tell them what to do. We hire smart people so they can tell us what to do."*
>
> ~STEVE JOBS

Trust in your teams from the start. Guide them and offer advice. Then allow them the space to grow and figure out the challenging situations that arise.

A LACK OF BELIEF CAN BE DESTRUCTIVE

While showing your team you believe in them and their abilities reinforces the brick of belief, acting like you do not believe in your team will degrade the bridge. When I have been micromanaged in my past roles, I felt unheard and undervalued and thus uninspired. In speaking with others, they have seen it the same way.

"When you are told exactly what to do and how to do it, why bring up new ideas?" a colleague asked me when we were discussing a former manager.

It frustrated him that our manager at the time was always detailing exactly how each step of the project needed to happen. The manager had just asked all of us to bring ideas to the table for the next step in the process. She didn't realize how ironic the question was, given that she always went ahead with her ideas and did not listen to our ideas.

It all stems from a lack of trust and belief in what the person or team can bring to the table or what they can become.

Let's look at this story about Savannah to see what can happen.

Most days Savannah loved working for the tech company. The products she worked on touched the lives of millions of customers. It was an exciting career she had created over the past several years, but Savannah's manager did not provide her with space to grow.

One part of her job was to present marketing plans and strategies to top executives. She worked diligently to make sure she dotted every i and crossed every t. Prior to each of the meetings with the executives, Savannah would go through her presentation with her manager, Evelyn. She would ask to hear every word Savannah was going to say and then would criticize each and every word.

"No, you can't use that word with Sam. It would trigger him, and then the entire presentation will spiral," Evelyn said, only a few slides in.

Each time this happened, Savannah felt more and more angst about the presentation.

During one presentation, Savannah felt Evelyn's eyes shooting daggers at her as she was presenting.

Had I said something incorrectly? she wondered.

This happened so often Savannah began to get hives before each presentation. She became so focused on what she could not say and the tone to use and not use that she was getting lost entirely. She found herself losing her voice. Nearly everything from her manager focused on the negative and what was wrong.

Every time she practiced a presentation, all she could think was, *This isn't going well. Where is she going to be upset?*

Her manager turned this incredible growth opportunity into something Savannah dreaded. She felt like she was being graded but without much possibility of passing, let alone succeeding. By not believing in Savannah, Evelyn limited the space Savannah could grow into. With each word, she showed Savannah she did not believe in her.

The key is to offer guidelines and suggestions to your employees or team, as well as to give them the space to grow and find their leadership style and voice.

BELIEF FROM YOUR MANAGER CAN BE INSPIRING
In prior chapters, we discussed my first manager, Stephen. From the very start, he saw the raw potential in me, and not just in the role I was in. He told me he wanted to support my growth—in research skills as well as soft skills. He helped me to excel in my ability to analyze consumer research data and create a multi-variant pricing study, to tell stories from the research data, to read a room while presenting, and so much more.

Stephen clearly was building his side of the bridge with his belief in me, and I worked even more diligently on my part of the bridge. Stephen offered opportunities and challenged me to grow into them. He would find complicated projects for me to take on. He would push me to outline the research plan first and then come to him for advice. He looked for assignments that would stretch me to grow in ways I didn't know initially if I could reach. He was always there to encourage me to stretch into whatever the new assignment called for. Because of that, I worked hard to grow into the next level he saw for me.

I once worked on an in-home use test (IHUT) where consumers took a well-known dressing (a current version and potential new version) as well as competitive products home for two weeks to try them out. The research was blind, which meant the users did not know which ranch dressing they had. When the research came back, the results were not clear-cut.

After analyzing the data and going back to Stephen with the results and my recommendation, we walked through my analysis together with Stephen asking multiple questions along the way. I took copious amounts of notes, impressed by the pieces of the story or the analysis that Stephen deconstructed and then reconstructed. I soaked up every bit of his knowledge. He didn't step in and take over finishing up how the presentation should be created. He did not tell me that he needed to present the recommendation to the cross-functional team and management. Instead, he affirmed his belief in me by having me rework the recommendation and then present it to the full team. It would have been quicker and easier for him to take control. Instead, I learned a great deal from his questions and how to create the story for a recommendation.

Over time, I challenged myself to think about any question Stephen would ask before I went to him with a draft of a recommendation for a research plan or the results.

- *What should the story be?*
- *Does it all hang together? (the flow, supporting data, graphics)*
- *Who are the stakeholders in the audience?*
- *What questions will they and others ask?*
- *What will they want to know about the analysis?*
- *How will I respond?*

The more I worked on this, the more I grew in my role.

What I learned from Stephen is that you can grow people into what you see for them by your belief in them.

YEARS OF EXPERIENCE ARE NOT A PREREQUISITE FOR BELIEF

While CJ and Savannah were seasoned employees, that is not a prerequisite for having a belief in someone. When I worked with Stephen, I only had one year of professional work experience.

In the spring of 2012, Max was twenty-seven when he started working on the marketing team at a high-growth tech company. Just out of undergraduate school, he wanted meaningful assignments. When his employer tapped him to work on a major launch with a high-visibility project after being there for a few years, he was ecstatic. He knew this project would be high stakes and threw himself into it. Any part he could play in this launch would be noteworthy.

As the project progressed and the launch date drew closer, his manager, Josh, brought him into more and more meetings to shadow him and learn. One day, Josh told Max he would head up a key part of the project.

In the very next meeting, he let the team know: "Max is the owner of this."

The team discussed milestones and the key details for the project to be successful. At the end of the meeting, Josh again clarified, "Max is the point of contact on this, and he'll drive it."

Max had been with the company long enough to know what a big signal that was. People would now go to him for the key pieces. He would shepherd this part of the project along. Several weeks later, there was a meeting with the executives to discuss the launch.

"Max, you're going to drive the agenda. You'll present," Josh said two days before the executive meeting. Josh gave suggestions about what to do during the presentation. "This is your show. You run with it."

Those words showed Max how much belief Josh had in him. Max was running the project. Quite often, at this company, it was only leaders that presented. His manager, Josh, could have taken all the glory with this project, which would have been the norm. In this company, if Max had failed, Josh would have looked very bad. Instead, his manager brought him in and empowered him. He created an opportunity for Max to grow and learn. This was an opportunity to soar.

Max walked into the conference room with the executives feeling fully prepared. He nailed the presentation.

"Max and the team have done a great job of putting this together," Josh said at the conclusion of the presentation.

The executives nodded in agreement.

As with all launch meetings, some things needed to be updated and changed. The overall feedback was positive for what they had been working on. Looking back, one reason Max felt so calm and prepared was that he knew Josh had his back in case something went amiss.

This experience left Max, at age twenty-seven, with the knowledge and confidence he could present well to top executives. Max consistently stepped up for Josh. He continued to build his side of the bridge in each of their interactions. He believed Josh had his best interests at heart and would offer him opportunities for growth. This experience and many more with Josh led Max to where he is today, head of product at a high-growth start-up.

THE MULTIPLIER EFFECT OF BELIEF

"Leadership is unlocking people's potential to become better."

~BILL BRADLEY, DEMOCRATIC SENATOR AND
FORMER PROFESSIONAL BASKETBALL PLAYER

Giving Max the spotlight and the support helped him become a better leader. Max leveraged this when he became a manager, deciding he wanted to give opportunities to his team and focus on how to grow them.

Ninety days into his Head of Product position, Max was creating the definitive product strategy. He wanted to present it at the first quarterly product strategy meeting, which would be a few weeks away in July. Max knew with the initial development, there were two ways to do it and he weighed the options in his head:

Option 1: I can present to my peers and then give my team the information after the meeting.

Option 2: My team presents, and they have an incredible opportunity to grow and learn as well as hear feedback firsthand.

He chose the second option.

While Max sketched out an initial skeleton of the presentation and the strategy, he had the team review and fill in the rest. He didn't want them to be order takers. He wanted to know their thoughts. He wanted to grow them. The product team and the design team each crafted a ten-slide presentation on what their team was working on for the quarter. During the strategy meeting, Max planned to begin with overarching thoughts and have the rest of the team come in. He wanted to provide opportunities for them to be front and center.

Thinking back to his make-or-break moment with the launch, Max thought:

This is either going to go really well, or it is going to go completely off the rails, depending on how they take it.

The team met often, spending the next couple of weeks working on the slides and rehearsing the presentations. The day of the strategy meeting, Max began with his opening comments. He then passed it off to Fred, who was lead on the product. Next, Sylvia, who was the lead on design, presented all of her slides seamlessly. She handled the questions that came up as they had practiced. They planned the meeting for two hours, and it ended up going over.

After everyone signed off the Zoom call, the CEO and a couple of executives debriefed. All feedback was extremely positive.

"Max, that went very well," noted the CEO, Rom, known for being brusque and brutally honest. "One thing—Sylvia's deck was very buttoned up and crisp. She did an incredible job."

That was a high compliment from him as he gave compliments very sparingly. The presentation became the standard for how they present at each quarterly meeting now.

Some managers think they must be the ones to present. If not, why are they there? Will people wonder what I am doing here? Or they feel the need to present out of a space of wanting the accolades.

By having your team present and do well, it looks good for you as a manager. My philosophy of managing has always been: Shine the spotlight on the team. Through talking to numerous leaders and in my own experience, the added benefit is the spotlight also ends up shining on you.

How do you want your team to be?

HOW TO BUILD BELIEF AS A MANAGER:

- Pick projects for people that will give them opportunities to shine. If this is not possible, discuss how they can be as involved as possible. Think about ways to highlight their contributions.
- To set up your employee for success, provide the context needed to understand the opportunity.
- Define the expectations—goals, review cycle, how to provide status updates, etc. In doing this, you are partnering with your employee to ensure that they and the project are successful in this opportunity.
- Give them space to find their voice.
- Give them proper credit. All too often, I have seen managers that take credit for the hard work of someone on their team. When your team does well and you shine the light on them to your management, the light also shines brightly on you and your talent as a manager.
- Help your employees find ways to get out of their comfort zone and try new things. Be supportive and allow for mistakes.

HOW TO BUILD BELIEF AS AN EMPLOYEE:
- Have a growth mindset with your manager. Understand where they are exploring their leadership style.
- Provide them feedback to refine their leadership style so it works for you and the rest of the team. It is harder to improve if they don't know the areas they need to improve.
- When given these opportunities, understand the metrics used to determine the success of the project. Manage to those metrics to continue to build the belief your manager has in you.
- Ask for the opportunities you would like to have.
- Step into the open spots or potential places where you see a need for improvement. Create a plan to show how this is helpful. Align with your manager on the goals and expectations.
- Send bullets to your manager about how the project is progressing. These are bullets that your manager can send on to their manager to make them look great, which is always helpful for you (as well as your manager).

Belief begets belief. This brick builds on the foundational bricks of respect, trust, and connection, thereby strengthening the bridge.

In the next chapters, we will explore additional bricks, which can support rebuilding the bridge—*culture of curiosity*, *actively listening*, and *ownership with consistency*. With these three, the relationship can be even stronger.

PART 3:

MAINTAIN (OR REBUILD) FOR THE LONG TERM

> *"Building and repairing relationships are long term investments."*
>
> ~STEPHEN R. COVEY

Challenges and conflicts occur in all relationships. How you choose to meet these situations and maintain the relationship matters.

With the act of maintaining or rebuilding the relationship, you are recreating the trust, respect, and connection—the foundation of the bridge—with the other person.

To do this, we will focus on the following three bricks: culture of curiosity, actively listening, and ownership with consistency.

CULTURE OF CURIOSITY

Creating a culture of curiosity enables both sides to come together with ideas and explore them. Asking questions that support this discovery can unify both sides. We'll look at ways to ask the questions to encourage curiosity.

ACTIVELY LISTENING
When each side listens to understand the other fully, each feels seen and heard. With actively listening, we'll look at the three levels of listening and how this can help both sides navigate conflict and create a bond through conversation, thus maintaining the bridge.

OWNERSHIP WITH CONSISTENCY
Ownership with consistency will focus on creating a shared understanding of what happened to cause the conflict. By aligning on this and owning your part, both sides can move forward. Consistency is important because it demonstrates these are not empty words but rather future promises that are proven out with your actions.

To maintain or rebuild, you must act in a genuine and authentic way. If not, the bridge will just crumble away again.

Tracy had a manager at a large technology company, Lexa, who tried rebuilding relationships with her team. Lexa had damaged trust with the team by not following through with her commitments, micromanaging them, and demanding they work long hours on the weekend—when she did not. Her attempt was inauthentic.

Monday morning Lexa would ask how the weekend was. Midway through Tracy's first sentence about her fun weekend, Lexa would walk away or interrupt abruptly to discuss a work assignment and its deadline. It seemed as if someone in HR had instructed Lexa to ask about the weekend before jumping into work topics. By walking away or interrupting,

Tracy felt Lexa did not really care. This does not build trust, respect, or a connection.

In contrast, think of a manager who asks you about your weekend and genuinely wants to know about it. Think about the coffee klatch where they talk about anything but work. These actions build camaraderie, trust, respect, and a connection in the most genuine way.

When someone's questions are genuine (in a culture of curiosity) and they want to mend the relationship, there is eye contact when you're talking, staying focused on you instead of multitasking with emails or text messages (signs of actively listening). Complete this by owning any misstep you have had in the relationship and follow it up with consistent action in line with what you say, and you will maintain the bridge.

CHAPTER 8:

Culture of Curiosity

"Part of being successful is about asking questions and listening to the answers."

~ANNE BURRELL

Remember when you were young, and your mom or dad asked you to make your bed before school? Later that day, your parent would ask:

"Why wasn't the bed made this morning?"

Do you remember how you felt at that moment?

Often people start with *why* questions when they want to know more. The challenge with this question is that it comes off as accusatory. People are then quick to become defensive, whether you made your bed or not.

It is hard to have a tone of curiosity with *why* questions because there is an underlying "well, it should have been done" tone.

TO LISTEN WITH CURIOSITY, CHANGE THE WAY YOU ASK QUESTIONS

On the other hand, if you change a question to begin with *what* or *how*, you can more easily add a tone of curiosity and give the other person the sense that you are listening to them and want to understand. When you damage trust and connection, showing you want to understand the other side is a solid step to maintaining the bridge.

Sometimes the relationship between an employee and manager deteriorates, and it can feel impossible for each to understand the other side. If they lose trust, respect, and connection—or any of the three—in the tension and conflict, rebuilding them can feel like a lost cause. With the right approach to how they communicate with each other, the bridge can be rebuilt.

In this chapter, we'll explore how to ask questions that will facilitate understanding the other side—manager or employee—and strengthening the relationship. Asking questions increases the trust and connection as well as shows you have respect for whomever you are talking to, all of which contribute to a healthier work relationship and environment.

CREATE A CULTURE OF CURIOSITY

According to the 2018 *Harvard Business Review* article, "The Business Case for Curiosity," Francesca Gino conducted a survey of more than three thousand employees across a wide variety of industries and firms:

- Ninety-two percent credited curious people with bringing new ideas into teams and organizations and viewed curiosity as a catalyst for job satisfaction, motivation, innovation, and high performance.
- Only 24 percent reported feeling curious in their jobs on a regular basis.
- Roughly 70 percent stated that they face challenges in asking more questions at work.

One of the barriers this study found was while many employees claim to want time to be more curious, doing so means challenging the status quo and potentially coming up without a solution.

Being curious, especially in a relationship, is important.

When I interviewed Jennifer Moss, author of *The Burnout Epidemic*, we discussed how to create a culture of curiosity that encourages questions. By asking questions where you explore, you gain insight into the other person, which will either deepen the connection to maintain the bridge or help to rebuild the bridge.

A colleague, Michelle, once told me about a negotiation class she attended. They divided the class into pairs and gave each side a task to negotiate for. In the end, Michelle and her partner, Bob, both came away empty-handed. They were both negotiating for an orange. Neither one realized one needed the rind, and one needed the orange slices. They could have both achieved their goals if they had asked each other questions to discover what the other truly wanted. In the end, Michelle realized this was not an exercise to see who would *win* in the negotiation. It was an exercise to see how everyone could get what they needed. Success does not have to be a zero-sum game.

FINDING COMMON GROUND

Morgan was working for the State Treasury Department. Two people on his team were collaborating on a report. Their communication was off, and they were having some challenges resolving it. Instead of addressing the issues head-on, they began to nitpick at each other's parts of the report. Then the conversation moved to each of them saying personal things out of frustration. The situation was escalating.

Morgan brought Mary and Rosa into a conference room to discuss the situation. Before he even broached the subject of the conflict, he took a different tack. In getting curious and asking some questions, Morgan realized they were not hearing or respecting each other. He knew they needed to start at another place before they could discuss the report.

"I understand you both are frustrated," he began, noting that each of them was sitting with their arms crossed, neither one looking right at the other. "Let's start with something a little different before we dive into the topic. Let's do a bit of a game. What do you appreciate about each other?"

When both were silent, Morgan stepped in. "How about if I start?"

He then proceeded to list things he liked about Mary. As she listened, her frustration eased and so did her crossed arms.

"I like how you show up each day with a smile as well, Mary," Rosa chimed in.

"Well, you are pretty great at analytics, Rosa," Mary added, who then listed other things she appreciated about Rosa.

Both had then moved to noting work-related characteristics about each other.

Within a few minutes, Morgan had helped them find common ground about things they appreciated about the other. This allowed them to pause, reflect, and move from a defensive standpoint to a place where they were open to considering the other person's standpoint on the situation.

When they then moved to talk about the project and where they felt frustration, they were much more open and curious. They were able to hear each other.

When you start from a base of curiosity, it changes the whole dynamic of the conversation. It starts from a base of trust and respect. Finding the characteristics you value about the other person adds respect as well as connection, which is now stronger. With a culture of curiosity, when your team members have a conflict again, it likely will not escalate.

In talking to Mary and Rosa about what is important to them about the report with open-ended questions, Morgan found out Mary really wanted the report to include her analysis, and Rosa needed the report to be presented in a certain way.

Both were possible.

> *"Most people do not listen with the intent to understand. They listen with the intent to reply."*
>
> ~STEPHEN R. COVEY

This is exactly what Mary and Rosa had moved to. They were so frustrated with each other that they were not listening with any curiosity. They were only listening enough to poke holes and refute the other's argument.

While this story includes two employees, notice how the manager brought them together and leveraged questions to engage them both, create connection, and hold space for them to diffuse the argument. A conflict between an employee and manager can also be resolved in this same manner.

Any *why* question can become a *what* or *how* question.

THREE MAGIC WORDS CAN CHANGE SO MUCH

With a culture of curiosity, you can also leverage questions to create more creative solutions.

Several years ago, when I worked at Plantronics, we were sitting in a massive room of a creative agency in Palo Alto. While I don't remember the product we were brainstorming, I do remember the session.

If you know much about creative agencies, brainstorming is a common activity. When a company is looking for solutions, agencies often start with brainstorming, where everyone in the group generates a wide variety of potential ideas to solve a given challenge or problem.

We were stuck trying to figure out how to create some packaging. We'd been talking about it for some time.

Suddenly, the moderator said these three incredible words, "How might we?"

These three words changed the course of the entire session. We set aside the ways we had previously created the packaging. We found new, creative ideas for the packaging material, the enclosure, and the messaging.

I started using these three words when working with others and when managing people. I also used them to manage up. In all situations, using these words changes the conversation.

What I love about these words is they unlock creativity and possibility on both sides. Let's break it down.

- **How:** The word *how* opens up a world of creativity—coming up with potential ideas, solutions, or even new perspectives on the situation at hand.

- **Might:** The word *might* opens up a world of possibility. We are not saying *will* as in this is the one and only way to do it. There is no deviation from this plan. We are not using *should*. There is not a value judgment on it. Instead, with the word *might*, we are building on the creativity from *how* and adding in *possibility,* which makes it even stronger in the world of coming up with ways to look at the current situation.

- **We:** The word *we* indicates this is something we want to partner with the other person on. We are on the same side of the table with them instead of sitting across from them. We will look at the situation together.

HOW MIGHT WE...

This beautiful three-word start to a question works in a multitude of settings. It works if you are talking to your employee and want to support them in learning how to think more broadly about how to find solutions instead of just delegating the task to them. You can follow it up with "what challenges might arise?" Or "who might we need to include in this decision?"

It also works well if you are talking to your manager about something and want some guidance. If you are talking about workload, you could use the "how might we" question to define what stays and what goes above and below the waterline—what projects you have the bandwidth for and which may need to be sidelined for a bit. I have done this often with my managers as well as with my team.

When I worked at Logitech, we had an incredible opportunity to be a part of the first-ever Amazon Alexa Smart Home table placed in a prominent, highly trafficked part of the Best Buy stores. The price tag to participate was massive and would have taken a disproportionate amount of our budget.

I pulled together my team, which was originally split on whether the investment of these funds would make sense. In brainstorming, I leveraged these three magical words. We figured out a way potentially to make it work and found numerous benefits, including more than just revenue, that would help us.

I have also used this in talking with an employee about how to overcome a challenge he was facing on a project. Asking a question with these three words and then listening to the other person opens up the conversation in an entirely new way because you are partnering together.

WORKING TO REBUILD THE BRIDGE

With several years of experience in sales and marketing, Collette came into work on hardware as a general manager at a high-growth start-up that would later become a Fortune 500 company. At the time, the company was transitioning its strategic focus from a hardware-based revenue stream to longer term hardware and software-as-a-service (SaaS) focus.

The challenge, however, was that the company's founder previously made all the decisions, especially around the product. Kai found it hard to let go of the product and roadmap decision-making.

Collette and Kai soon had ongoing disagreements about what would be on the product roadmap, what would launch, the timing of launches, and how the launch would work.

Collette found these constant disagreements challenging, as she is a driver they hired to be the general manager (GM) and own those decisions. Not owning the decisions reduced the scope of the position.

To Kai's credit, he recognized what was happening. He tried to let go of the decision-making, but it was hard for him. He consistently would step in.

During one meeting, Kai blew up at her in front of others, insisting they create the roadmap his way, and not how Collette was proposing.

The lack of alignment and trust caused fissures in their bridge, which led to its deterioration.

Because having a solid relationship as GM and CEO was important to both Collette and Kai, they met every Tuesday for lunch at a sushi restaurant away from the rest of the team to discuss how to work together in an effort to rebuild the bridge.

At each lunch, Kai listened to Collette, asking questions to further the dialogue. Collette did the same.

"What's working? And also, what's not working in our relationship?" Kai inquired.

"I want to own the product decisions of the roadmap. I want to feel trusted in the meetings to move forward with my recommendations."

They also sought to realign expectations.

"Okay. And what are you expecting?" Kai began in between bites of his California roll and sashimi.

"I make the decisions of what to launch and when. I am the GM." Collette said.

"Hmmm... I know this ecosystem so well. I know what we need, and I know when we need it."

Kai felt Collette wanted to own everything too quickly.

While they were out of alignment about who would have the final say in the decisions, they did learn how to disagree in a more constructive instead of destructive manner by asking for feedback and incorporating this manner into their interactions with each other. These conversations enabled them to rebuild the bridge, maintain it, and have more healthy dialogue at work.

After several months of these lunch conversations with great communication back and forth, Collette concluded this GM position was not the right one for her, as she and Kai fundamentally differed on what her role would be at the time. She ultimately decided to leave the company.

While some of the conversations did become heated and bumpy, they both always respected each other's opinions and continued to be curious about the other's point of view. They genuinely tried to come together. By asking questions, staying curious, and looping back to seek more feedback weekly, they were able to rebuild and then maintain their relationship.

By building the bridge back, they were able to leave with a bridge intact. As a manager, it is best to have an employee feel solid about you and the company when they leave. As an employee, you also want the manager to feel solid about you. Enabling people to part with mutual dignity and respect is important.

Both sides were able to find a way for Collette to leave with respect and dignity.

Even though the bridge deteriorated, and they were not on the same page, they were able to build it back by asking questions, being open, and staying curious. As well, they really listened to each other and accepted feedback from the other. These bricks we will discuss in the next chapter.

From this experience, Collette learned to communicate her expectations, make sure those expectations were aligned for future roles, and ask questions to move the conversation forward. She also realized how important it is to have respect for the other person and to have that person respect her.

In her future roles, Collette made sure she was clear on the expectations of the duties of the role for those she hired, and she did the same for future roles when she was interviewing. She also made sure to ask questions to create and rebuild strong relationships with her employees as well as her manager.

HOW TO BUILD A CULTURE OF CURIOSITY AS A MANAGER AND AN EMPLOYEE:

- Ask "How" and "What" questions instead of "Why" questions.

- Leverage the three magic words of "How might we" to collaborate better.

- Ask for feedback. How to ask about feedback:
    - "What do you need from me to be successful?"
    - "How can I support you in your role?"
    - "What's one thing you see me doing or not doing where I'm getting in my own way?"
    - These questions work for either the employee or manager.
    - Note: We'll talk more about feedback in the next chapter.

Being curious and asking questions is only part of the journey to rebuild the bridge. The next part of this is to listen well, which we will explore in the next chapter.

CHAPTER 9:

Actively Listening

"The most basic of all human needs is to understand and be understood. The best way to understand people is to listen to them."

~RALPH NICHOLS

"Ich bin ein Berliner."

No, I'm not talking about John F. Kennedy's speech in West Berlin. Eva, my good friend, had piped up to answer Herr Kauffmann's question at the start of our German poetry class during my undergraduate junior year. In all honesty, I had been focusing on understanding what Goethe had meant in the poem assigned to us.

Only half-listening, I had burst into giggles, imagining Eva as a jelly donut. ("Ich bin ein Berliner" translates to "I am a jelly donut" in German.)

The stern stare of Herr Kauffmann and slight nod of his head, highlighting his utter disapproval of my outburst in class, quickly silenced me. Had I not looked up, I would not have known he was so upset.

Message and meaning can be mixed up through translation (as with the jelly donut) if we are only listening to the literal words said rather than being crystal clear if we are listening and paying attention to all the clues (both verbal and nonverbal).

Often in the workplace, people still believe listening is one-sided. One person talks, and *they* (either the employee or the manager) do not really listen.

Listening requires both sides. Without listening actively, we can damage the relationship in terms of trust, respect, connection, boundaries, and alignment, which can be quite detrimental. The converse is also true. Actively listening can strengthen trust, respect, connection, boundaries, and alignment—all the parts of the relationship.

Actively listening enables feedback and conflict management, leading to healthier teams. Listening is giving one's thoughtful and considerate attention to another. It is more than just hearing someone. You have to go deeper.

According to the Co-Active Training Institute's book, *Co-Active Coaching: The Proven Framework for Transformative Conversations at Work and in Life*, listening has three levels.

LEVEL ONE

Level One listening is listening mostly to yourself. This can be your own thoughts or agenda. Some examples include when you're in a conversation and you're thinking about what to say next, which may also mean you are not fully listening to what the other person's saying. Or while listening to someone, your stomach is grumbling, and then you start to consider what to have for lunch or if you left the lights on at home. In Level One listening, you're not fully hearing what the other person is saying.

LEVEL TWO

With Level Two listening, you focus on what the other person is saying without other thoughts distracting you. You are hearing all the words the other person is saying, and you are present. This is an example of *not* listening to respond but rather listening to hear what the other person has to say before deciding on your response.

LEVEL THREE

With Level Three listening, your focus remains completely directed toward the other person, as with Level Two. However, you are hearing more than just the words. You notice the other person's body language, the inflections and tone of their voice, and when they pause or if they hesitate. Instead of a smaller laser focus, it is as if you have widened the focus. You hear (and in some ways can sense) the whole of them. I'm referring to the nonverbal cues. Think about when you have been talking to someone, and they start avoiding eye contact or heave a deep sigh. At Level Three, you key in on those things as well.

A MIX OF ALL THREE LEVELS OF LISTENING

Active listening can support you as both a manager and an employee to know others on a deeper level. Level One can also be listening to your gut intuition. Active listening is a crucial skill in many different parts of the relationship between manager and employee. Here are the biggest places:

- Conflict Management and Resolution
- Feedback

From previous chapters, we know people have been working harder and longer hours during the pandemic. Active listening helps them feel heard and valued.

Pam was working in human resources at a large manufacturing company when a challenging employee relations concern popped up. Her manager, Frank, was in another country. They had been going back and forth on how to approach the issue. Eventually, they reached a decision regarding how to address it.

"So, we're in a good place, and we can now send this out?" Pam asked.

"Yes. Looks great to me."

Pam was glad she had his agreement, as she knew this was a delicate situation. She reread the communication once more and then pushed send.

Unfortunately, Frank did not discuss and align the decision with upper management (those above him), which turned the issue into a very challenging situation in the organization. Her manager ended up telling the rest of management that Pam had made the decision on her own, even though she had not.

Later that week, Frank and Pam were on a Zoom call he had set up, and he was quiet during the majority of the call. They sat there for thirty minutes, silently. Pam didn't even know until several days later, from other coworkers, that the Zoom call was to have been a corrective action discussion.

Pam learned so many lessons from Frank during her time working under him. Many of them are positive lessons that changed how she manages to this day. From this experience, however, she not only learned how important it is to document and not have blind faith, but also how important it is to rebuild trust and respect if it is broken.

In this case, Frank chose not to work on rebuilding trust. There was no discussion, no questions, and thus no listening. He lost her respect and trust. They were never as close as they were before.

Pam decided when she makes a mistake, it is crucial to own her part with her employees (or with her manager). Knowing how the situation affected her, Pam works to ensure trust and respect remain intact. She does this by really listening to what her team is saying and not saying. She pays attention to their tone, body language, and other nonverbal cues.

Many view conflict as challenging or something to avoid. With listening and trust, conflict can make a relationship even stronger.

CONFLICT CAN STRENGTHEN A RELATIONSHIP

Maxine had been working for a global manufacturing organization for a few years. Like Pam, she worked in HR. She and Ryan, her manager, had worked together for several months and had built a solid relationship.

Maxine thought the process for certain tasks was counterproductive and didn't make sense. She and Ryan differed on how the process should go. Maxine is very comfortable in her skin. She's fine to challenge things if she does not agree with how they are.

In previous conversations, it would go something like this:

"Ryan, I don't think it should go like this," explained Maxine.

He would disagree. They would go back and forth a bit.

"Maxine, this is my decision to make. You know this, right?" said Ryan.

When she approached Ryan about these processes, she braced herself to be frustrated and for Ryan to be frustrated, as had happened a few times in the past. The conversation went differently this time.

"I'm glad we have a chance to talk about this. I know we disagree," Ryan began.

Here it comes, she thought.

"Tell me how you view the situation. What's your base of information? I'm wondering what you are considering."

Maxine explained why she believed the process to be counterproductive. Ryan listened intently to what she was saying.

"Ah, okay, well, let me fill in some missing pieces for you," Ryan said.

He provided some context and then asked what Maxine thought. After that, he provided more information and context. He didn't give it to her all at once. He just kept expanding for her, and then he would check in with her about her thoughts.

This is a great example of Level Two listening.

At some point, she understood where he was coming from. He must have noticed she relaxed her brow as she had been considering things in her head.

Noticing her facial expression is a great example of Level Three listening.

Just then, Ryan asked, "So what do you think now? What decision would you make now?"

"I would make the same decision you are suggesting."

Maxine always remembered this exchange. It was a turning-point conversation. She hadn't felt overruled or undermined. It wasn't confrontational. It was respectful to her. Ryan understood the reason they were disagreeing was that Maxine was missing some information. Potentially, with this information, Maxine would have changed her mind. The same could be true of Ryan.

This is why coming together to work through a conflict with solid listening skills is helpful. Conflict is not necessarily bad. Ryan's approach of asking Maxine what context she had, determining she might be missing some key information, and providing that to her changed Maxine's whole view of Ryan as a leader.

This conversation felt inclusive and collaborative. By giving Maxine more context, she felt more engaged than she had in prior discussions. With this way of navigating conflict, Maxine could own the decision more. She could implement it with confidence. When she shared it with the organization, she felt like it was the right thing to do, which changes everything how other people experience what you're working on.

This conversation turned a relationship that was beginning to have some challenges into a stronger one.

Often, with conflict, we can start to lose trust. Having open communication with transparency and active listening can rebuild trust and strengthen the relationship.

FEEDBACK IS A TWO-WAY STREET

Giving and receiving feedback is a crucial skill. While there are corporate trainings on how to give feedback, many do not incorporate active listening. Nearly always, these feedback trainings skip over the part about *receiving* the feedback. The key is not just in giving the feedback but also in receiving the feedback as well. We will begin with how to give feedback, and then cover how to receive feedback.

Giving feedback is divided into two sections: How and What

HOW OF GIVING FEEDBACK: THE PAN METHOD

To give feedback, I created an acronym: PAN: public/private, actionable, now.

- **Public/Private:** If the feedback is negative, then it is, of course, better to be in private than in person. If the feedback is positive, it can be great to give feedback publicly. However, some people enjoy public praise whereas others prefer to have praise in private instead. Talk to your team about how they want to receive feedback. Providing feedback the way they want to receive it is another way of listening to them. When you are providing feedback, whether it is public or private, pay attention to their nonverbal cues (Level Three listening) to ensure they are receiving the feedback in the manner you intend it to be received. Sometimes asking questions here can be helpful to confirm that their understanding is in sync with the message you intend to deliver.

- **Actionable:** The feedback needs to detail specifics. If it is too generic, people will not know what they need to do next. This goes for feedback you are giving to an employee as well as giving feedback to your manager.

- **Now:** Giving the feedback immediately enables the situation to be fresh in both your mind and the mind of the receiver. This also helps with the ability to recall specifics. Do not sacrifice giving the feedback in person in favor of speed. It is always important to give feedback (positive or constructive) in person (or live video if you are remote or hybrid).

WHAT OF GIVING FEEDBACK: SITUATION—BEHAVIOR—IMPACT

Let's break down the concept of helpful feedback into three components: situation, behavior, and impact.

- **Situation:** First, detail what was happening. Talk about the circumstances of the situation and who was involved.

- **Behavior:** Next, look at what the person did in the situation. What was the action? What was their part in the situation?

- **Impact:** Lastly, explain what the impact was on the other person. Ask what the intention was of the receiver. People rarely have bad intentions. People with great intentions have bad impacts all of the time. This is another place to pull in the Level Three listening skills. Potentially, people can become defensive here. Walk through both sides of the intentions. What were the intentions of the person you are speaking with? What may the other person have felt as an impact? Notice how we are again using *what* questions here.

When you walk through feedback this way, it provides the feedback receiver the information they need to understand what is happening and how to change the situation for the future.

Feedback is often something people want, as many want to grow, learn, and improve in their career. However, they also want to be accepted and seen in a good light.

Sheila Heen, Harvard Law Faculty and coauthor of *Thanks for the Feedback: The Science and Art of Receiving Feedback Well*, details the many reasons for improving this skill in her 2015 TEDx talk. According to Heen, people who handle feedback better:

... have higher work satisfaction, adapt more quickly in new roles, and get higher performance reviews. When you get better at handling everybody's feedback for you, it doesn't just change you. It changes how other people see you and experience you.

Receiving and giving feedback can be a positive, productive act, and paired with actively listening, these are a critical part of rebuilding and strengthening the relationship between employee and manager.

> **HOW TO INTEGRATE ACTIVELY LISTENING FOR A MANAGER AND AN EMPLOYEE:**
> - Practice both Level Two and Level Three listening.
> - Provide context.
> - Ask *how* and *what* questions instead of *why* questions.
> - Leverage *how might we* to collaborate better.
> - Ask for feedback. Pose the following question to your team: "What's one thing you see me doing or failing to do where I'm getting in my own way?"
> - Listen for the message when you are receiving feedback.

Though it can be challenging to maintain or rebuild, it is vital to the relationship. Conflict is going to happen. In the hybrid world we often work in now, it is even more challenging. With a screen between people, it is too easy to miss nuanced nonverbal communication cues or subtleties in tone changes. People are sweeping this under the proverbial carpet and pushing the red *end call* Zoom button. You don't have to run into them in the office kitchen or the bathroom. Leaving conflict unresolved can cause challenges, which can also lead to impacting results. Pay attention to the nonverbal cues on Zoom—people pulling back in their chair, an exasperated sigh, folded arms. Then leverage curiosity and open-ended questions to understand what is happening for them.

CHAPTER 10:

Ownership with Consistency

"It is not only what we do, but also what we do not do, for which we are accountable."

~MOLIERE

The final brick critical to the repair of the bridge is a combination of ownership and consistency.

Think of this as an apology. If you apologize without any change, they are empty words. Ownership and a consistent change in action secure the bricks back into a solid place.

THE IMPORTANCE OF OWNERSHIP
In the example of the Actively Listening chapter with Pam and Frank, we saw how important ownership can be. In many ways, Frank missed an opportunity to rebuild the relationship when he did not own the mistake and talk to

Pam about what happened. Allowing the blame to fall on her when he had verbally authorized the communication deteriorated the trust.

Part of communicating is also being transparent and upfront. Frank could have communicated he needed more approvals before Pam could move forward. If, for some reason, he did not know at the moment, he could have owned it later during the *corrective action* call.

By sitting silently on the Zoom call, Frank was pretending, like an ostrich, to stick his head in the sand and imagine it did not happen. The lack of ownership created a situation where Frank and Pam were unable to loop back to create the trust that was already broken.

If, on the other hand, you own your part in whatever happened to breach the trust or respect, it becomes possible to move forward.

One or two incidents do not define you. It is when those incidents happen again and again that they become a pattern of behavior. With an incident or two, you can rebuild.

~ ~ ~ ~

When the bridge deteriorates, seek to understand the situation with curiosity (asking questions with an open mind) and listen actively, as we have discussed in the prior two chapters. In understanding how things fell apart, you can own your side. It is hard to own your part if you don't know what part you played.

What was the root of the problem? Was it one situation or was it a lack of small interactions to reinforce the bridge? Diagnose the cause with the other person involved. Have a discussion where you ask some open-ended questions, seek feedback, and listen to the other person.

Fully own how you contributed to the situation with humility and without excuses. Create a plan to rebuild trust, respect, and connection with the other person—your manager or employee. Through your actions, the other person—manager or employee—will see that you are genuine. Then the trust, respect, and connection will return.

Consistency is another important component to reestablish the bridge. As they say, the proof is in the pudding. You cannot expect miracles overnight, meaning the relationship will not change with one discussion. This is why being consistent with your actions is important.

TIME AND EXPERIENCE
Time and experience will provide evidence of the opinion your manager or employee has of you. First, whether you are maintaining or repairing the bridge, if you are consistent with your actions, you give the other person the time and experience to know they can and should believe that you will continue to do so, which then rebuilds the trust in you, respect they have for you, and connection with you.

Repeatedly observing challenging behavior problems reinforces a negative opinion.

Several years ago, I managed someone whom we will call Joe. Though he had incredible marketing ideas, he was consistently late with deliverables. He was short (and sometimes very critical publicly) with our counterparts, whom we needed to execute our marketing ideas, packaging, launches, etc. While I outlined clear expectations, they were not met. We discussed what would motivate him and chatted about whether this was the right fit for him. Neither of which led to a different outcome. Deliverables were still late, and his demeanor remained challenging for others.

During our one-on-one, he would say the right things:

- "I'm on it. I know this is important. I will have it done in two weeks."
- "I will chat with the team in a more inclusive way. I will dial back the biting sarcasm."

He did not, however, execute in this way.

Time plus experience reinforced our deteriorating bridge. I trusted him less and less to deliver, as he consistently missed deadlines, even though he provided the deadline.

When those incidents happen again and again, they become a pattern of behavior.

RESET TO REBUILD

A February 2020 article in the *Harvard Business Review* cited a large-scale review of three hundred studies published in management and psychology over the past fifteen years.

These studies focused on workplace relationships, relationship transgressions, and relationship repair. After this thorough review, researchers found some ways to help repair work relationships.

They suggest starting by *resetting the emotional tone*. To do this, immediately acknowledge the tension and allow each other to express negative feelings. Then emphasize positive feelings about the future of the relationship. Listen without being defensive. Commit to a shared relationship goal. Agree that your relationship is important and you both want to restore mutual positive feelings.

In addition to immediately acknowledging the tension and what happened, the researchers found that creating a shared narrative is one of the most important practices people in the workplace can do to mend a relationship. In having this, it increases people's willingness to forgive and rebuild the bridge if they assume the best (and not the worst) about the other person's intentions. This shared narrative enables both sides to see the other person's side. When doing this, start by asking about the other person's story about what happened and then offer your thoughts. Practice the active listening we discussed previously, without interrupting or becoming defensive. This shared narrative enables ownership by both sides.

CREATING SHARED UNDERSTANDING TO MOVE FORWARD

Denise was the director of fundraising for a prominent nonprofit. She had a meeting with one of the board members, Liz. During that meeting, they had some strategic discussions.

One of the ideas Liz proposed was unrealistic. It was something that would be cumbersome for the nonprofit to engage with and had a limited upside for the nonprofit. That said, there would be good visibility for Liz's organization.

Denise debriefed her manager, Natalia, on the way home, detailing the challenges with Liz's suggestion.

"Okay. Makes sense. That doesn't sound like a realistic thing we can do, Denise," Natalia agreed.

Later that week, Denise called the CEO, Toni, and also shared the update with her. Everyone was on the same page… or so Denise thought. Liz spoke with Toni, who then immediately called Denise.

"I just spoke with Liz, who said she has yet to receive an update on the project. She is under the impression you are going to implement her idea," Toni said.

"I'm sorry. I thought we were all on the same page that we would not pursue it because it did not make sense for us," Denise replied.

"Right, but you didn't fully close the loop with her. You need to be very clear with her on where we landed."

Toni was not mean to Denise. She was simply very firm.

"Liz is my stakeholder. She's my boss. You are my partner in this. I need to know you are communicating clearly with her," Toni explained.

Denise owned her part in the miscommunication when she spoke with Toni. Denise told Toni she should have been clearer with Liz. Toni explained her expectations, especially with such a high-profile relationship as the one with a board member, Liz.

There was no blame. Toni walked Denise through what should have happened. Through this discussion, they were able to create a shared narrative with ownership, as well as a clear sense of what should happen in the future.

"We don't need to hold on to this. Let's learn and move forward," were Liz's last words of their conversation that afternoon.

While some trust was broken in this situation, by Denise owning her part, they could move the focus to rebuild the trust, which they did. Toni had Natalia sit in on meetings for a while with Denise. Instead of feeling micromanaged, Denise took this as an opportunity to show Natalia and Toni they could trust her. Denise took copious notes and clarified the action items. She circled back diligently on post-meeting communication.

Now Denise always makes sure she has more frequent chats with her managers.

Through the ownership and the consistent actions, the bridge is now solid, with trust and respect back in place.

The more the relationship is damaged, the more you need to be consistent in rebuilding the trust, so the other person (manager or employee) will have faith that you will continue to be consistent.

EACH SITUATION IS AN OPPORTUNITY TO BUILD ON

I met with Andy Pray, CEO and Founder of Praytell, an incredible Public Relations and Media agency that won PRWeek's Best Place to Work in 2020 and was a finalist from 2014 to 2020, a remarkable seven years in a row. He did this by building a company with three main principles:

- Build an incredible community
- Create a company that fundamentally is one of consensus
- Run against the intensity and clarity of a deadline

As Andy began his career as a KPIX public media journalist in San Francisco, deadlines were critical to him, and he never lost that drive, which he now instills in all of his team at Praytell, headquartered in New York.

Andy and his leadership focused on fostering these bonds with people at work and in play. They have an annual offsite called Camp Praytell, which started when they were only twenty people and spent time together in the Catskills in New York. No work. A weekend of bonding. They continued this every year—even when they grew to be 175 people. Everyone attends this fun-filled weekend of games, campfires, skits, and so much more. They literally and figuratively built community through interaction.

"People see each other and remember that we're all humans. That commitment is something that will never go away."

Through 2020, the company didn't lay anyone off, though several other companies did. While they did put some on paid leave, they brought back all of those employees.

In the summer of 2021, for the first time in a number of years, Praytell began experiencing attrition. People were leaving for other places. They started hiring people quickly to fill holes. The formerly tight-knit community no longer felt that way anymore.

When they saw the attrition, they began to refocus on the company culture. Andy and the leadership team realized they were *talking* about community but not *upholding* this value as they wanted to. It is important to recognize as a manager or an employee when you are not "walking the talk," as they say. Looping back, talking to his executive team and owning the incongruence (not upholding the commitment of building community) was the first step.

During our interview for this book, Andy spoke about rebuilding a bridge and said, "It's about consistency, and it's about receipts."

Showing the receipts is a term that means you are providing evidence for doing what you are saying. By consistently *showing the receipts*, Andy and the leadership team rebuilt the trust and respect with the employees. They celebrated their people in big ways and small ways. They focused on reconnecting and creating the community they spoke about, and these actions of connection and community building rippled out to all managers and employees.

One of the primary ways Andy builds community as a company is with Camp Praytell, which they held again in 2022. The community of this company is now stronger than ever.

While this is a macro example, it exemplifies how you can rebuild the bridge. Since Praytell executed this companywide, you can also achieve these results as a manager or an employee.

While rebuilding may move more slowly than building the bridge initially, it remains critical to having solid relationships. Conflict and challenges will arise, which can test or fracture the bridge. Work relationships that have broken bridges make it much more difficult to do work when there is a lack of trust, respect, connection, curiosity, listening, and ownership. Rebuilding a bridge that is broken ensures you have both a bridge that is strong enough to endure as well happy, high-performing teams with happy, high-performing leaders.

HOW TO MAINTAIN THE BRIDGE WITH OWNERSHIP AND CONSISTENCY FOR A MANAGER AND AN EMPLOYEE:

- Create a shared narrative that both sides own and agree on
- Focus on ownership
    - What did you learn?
    - What will you do differently?
    - How can I make it right?

- Be consistent with your words and actions to rebuild
- Understand it may take time to rebuild the relationship

Next, we are going to look at some examples of incredible leaders people want to work for again and again. Leverage their ideas to become a great leader, or learn from what they love about the employees they continually want to hire at the next place they go.

PART 4:

THE SEARCH FOR THE UNICORN: LEADERS WHO LEAD AND INSPIRE

> "A good leader inspires people to have confidence in the leader, a great leader inspires people to have confidence in themselves."
>
> ~ELEANOR ROOSEVELT

Many can direct and delegate. Fewer can manage well. Even fewer still can lead and inspire.

During my research, I found some managers who were also leaders who lead and inspired.

- They focused on developing their people.
- Each had pillars or cornerstones they believe in for leading.
- Creating a bridge with their employees was a focus where they were proactive and intentional.
- The employees so loved working for them that they wanted to come back and work for them again and again.

Each of them has stories that highlight many of the bricks in building the bridge. While each chapter has highlighted an individual brick, the following leaders show how to bring them together to create a bridge.

- Krista Todd, Chief Marketing Officer (CMO) for NortonLifeLock
- Rodney Toy, Tech Executive and Adviser
- Stephen Bohnet, Founder at F'inn, a marketing research agency

"Your single biggest investment you can make is in yourself and in people."

~WARREN BUFFETT

All the leaders I interviewed firmly believe developing people is the best investment they can make as well as developing themselves. I theorized if you were a manager whom people love and wanted to work for wherever you went (a unicorn), maybe you had a unicorn for a manager.

I say unicorn because it is a mythical beast. Quite often, when I have asked people to tell me about the great managers they have had, they did not have an example. Some had singular stories. Very few had great managers who were great leaders who invested in them.

These three leaders are different from others because they had examples of a leader who invested in them and their development, and these three leaders also made it a priority to develop great leaders.

WHAT WE CAN LEARN FROM THESE LEADERS
When you put all the bricks together, as these leaders show, you enable the solid relationships that create happy, healthy teams. All of them build the foundation of trust, respect, and connection first.

With these examples, we see the importance of setting expectations and boundaries, achieving alignment, and providing opportunities and belief. Each of these further reinforces the bridge.

CHAPTER 11:

Leader #1 Stephen Bohnet

First, we will look at a leader who is charismatic, introverted, and very talented at connecting dots to tell compelling stories. Stephen Bohnet, Partner at F'inn has been managing for two decades. With a knack for seeing through complex data sets to find simple stories, Stephen looks at both the big picture and tactical sides of the issues. He has made a career of building great teams and believes everyone from the janitor to the CEO deserves the same amount of respect and dignity.

LEADER #1: STEPHEN BOHNET, PARTNER AT F'INN

HOW IT ALL BEGAN WITH TRUST AND BELIEF

After being at a market research company for a few years, Stephen's manager, Ed, asked Stephen to fly to Texas with him. Ed wanted to develop people who were great business thinkers as he considered most of the team to be focused only on spitting out figures and charts without being able to connect the numbers to a story. As part of developing the team, he gave them a great deal of independence.

Over dinner that night, Ed said, "Stephen, tomorrow you will be leading the presentation for Nokia."

Stephen was surprised, as this would be his first time presenting for Nokia. He stayed up all night practicing the presentation and nailed it the next day while Ed sat in the back of the room without saying anything.

Stephen was so well-prepared for this moment because for the two years prior, Ed and others had grilled him and challenged him on details. Stephen had enjoyed these challenges because he knew he became more adept in his position with each that he faced. They challenged him so he would be ready for this exact circumstance with Nokia. When a leader from Nokia had a question, Stephen knew the answers, spoke to all the data, and explained the recommendations.

Ed trusted in Stephen's ability so much so that he didn't need to step in. As we have talked about in other examples, Ed was exemplifying with his actions that Stephen was the one in charge of this meeting.

At F'inn, the market research firm that Stephen cofounded, Stephen has his team present. Even as the senior person in the room, he is not the first one to answer the questions. He wants the team to have an opportunity to answer.

Enabling your team members is core to their growth and helps them feel valued and appreciated. Empower your team.

Give them the tools that they need to be successful. Enable their success, which has multiple benefits—for them, you, and your relationship.

RESOLVE THE UNINTENTIONAL, INTENTIONALLY
Several years ago, Stephen lived and worked in Paris for a large market research firm. He traveled to Germany for a presentation to Braun, one of their top clients. The team talked about how to figure out the launch. The presentation went very well. The client was happy.

As Stephen was going to leave, Celeste, who had been working in the field department, stopped him. She was rather upset.

"You went up there and took all the credit. You answered all the questions," Celeste said.

She told him that he had made it sound like he was doing everything when she had been working hard on the ground on this project. Stephen listened to all of her concerns. Then they had an open discussion. She talked about how she felt and what she wanted. This led to a shared narrative between the two of them about what had happened and then created an opportunity for more conversation.

They discussed what being up in the front of the room and leading would entail, with Stephen outlining the expectations for her to be ready to be able to present in front of the room. Their discussion was collaborative, and they created a plan and an opportunity for her to present.

While he had not intentionally tried to damage the trust and respect he had with Celeste, Stephen had hurt the relationship. Had he not listened to her and had the open conversation, he could have damaged the relationship further. Given that they did not see each other regularly, he might not have known the extent of the damage. Stephen learned that how you show up can affect people in all sorts of ways. You have to be mindful in your position as a manager.

Listening, respecting her opinion, owning his part (and apologizing), and discussing what she wanted and what he needed (setting expectations) enabled them to build back quickly their relationship and to move forward on a surer footing.

This is why it is important to first have the trust, respect, and connection to create the space to have this conversation. Celeste talking about her frustration enabled Stephen to see the impact. As we talked about with feedback, sometimes people don't know the impact of their actions. Stephen did not have the intention of hurting Celeste.

Having conversations, even challenging ones, early on makes the repair of the relationship significantly easier.

THE POWER OF FLEXIBILITY
Core to Stephen's management style is his belief that you should always treat people with dignity.

When he was first starting out, he noticed the power dynamics of business. He observed other managers who acted as if they had the mentality of: *I don't need to change. I can manage it however I want.*

From his manager, Ed, he came to understand not everyone learns the same way. Managing a team, however you want without taking individual learning styles into account, is ultimately detrimental to the manager and the team. Stephen is a flexible manager who adapts to the needs of his team.

For example, he is very much a self-starter who does not need praise. In fact, he recalls that he did not internalize the praise that his managers gave him. In his mind, if no one told him he was doing something wrong, everything was fine. But he knows this approach does not work for everyone.

He provides praise more often to those that want it more frequently. This is important to him because he wants them to receive feedback often and know where they stand so reviews are never a surprise.

By understanding the motivation and the ways your team responds best—learning styles, feedback styles, communication, etc.—the easier it is to create and strengthen the relationship. This is true for both managers and employees. You can gather all of this information by knowing yourself and getting to know your employee, by asking open-ended questions, and by really listening to the answers.

THE ART OF SAYING HI
When I interviewed Stephen, we talked about connection and its importance in creating solid relationships between

employees and managers. He told me about how shy he was as a young child and teen. Stephen believes connection and human interaction are part of what makes work fun. He now goes into any room and walks up to people and says hi. He calls this "the art of saying hi" (the same tip we discussed in the Connection chapter.)

This act does not require much effort. Start with hi and ask the person some questions. Get to know them a bit. Stephen notes that if you walk into a room and don't strike up a conversation initially, it is awkward to want to do that an hour later when everyone else has already been talking.

The two puzzle pieces in this skill are desire and curiosity. You have to want to connect with someone.

Stephen has an insatiable sense of curiosity. You could start talking about any topic and he would be interested. He always wants to know more.

When he connects with his team, with vendors, or with prospective clients, he always starts by trying to find a point of connection. He says this is especially important if there is a challenging person. Find the connection with them on a human-to-human level. Then move into the business pieces. Whether getting to know someone on his team, a vendor, or a prospective client, the human interaction and connecting with others, getting to know their business, and supporting them to solve their business challenges—those are the pieces Stephen loves and is incredibly talented at.

Connecting in this way can build the foundation for your relationships as well. Pull from your curiosity and desire to connect with the other person. In doing this, you may likely learn more about them that you respect and admire or more reasons why you have more belief in them.

WORK CAN BE THROWN AWAY, RELATIONSHIPS AND IMPACT CANNOT

In the Fall of 2001, the economy had not been solid for a while. Clorox internally announced they would be having layoffs. They did not say when. The news hung in the air like a thick layer of fog in the marina during the morning. Week after week went by, and the layoffs did not happen. The chatter and speculation, literally the water cooler talk at the time, grew.

One day, Stephen noticed people walking out of a corner office near his cubicle. These were the same people Stephen had worked with or seen on the escalator as he was going to his desk. They, like him, had methodically organized all of their work for years.

He watched people walk out of the office, pack up their cubicles, and leave the building. They placed their belongings into a cardboard box and left.

Then others came into those cubicles and shredded all of the documents and files his friends and colleagues had spent so much time working on.

Someone's life's work is being thrown away, as if it does not count, Stephen thought.

That's when he realized someone could throw away his life's work, if he defined his life's work as the projects he had completed and filed. Prior to that fall day, he had already considered people to be important, but seeing the documents shredded or tossed out was a turning point for Stephen, where he decided to build his career around things others could not throw away.

When we were talking about relationships and their importance, Stephen said:

I'm building something that is lasting.

While he knows his research has saved corporations lots of money or made them lots of money over the years, that is not the most important thing for him.

"The only other things I'm building that's lasting are the relationship, the education, and the training for somebody to go on and succeed."

He focuses on helping his clients with their business challenges, redefining strategy and where to focus. Just as importantly, he wants to support them in achieving a promotion or in leading other businesses or teams. With his team at F'inn, his focus is growing them professionally as well as who they are as a whole person.

"What I want is to see a person go places and help them along the way. People I have managed have gone on to work at places like Microsoft, Apple, and Square."

He still has solid relationships with the people who have worked for him.

That is impressive bridge building, which also has a ripple effect. The leaders he helped nurture and create then go on to lead other teams and lead them with heart and empathy the way that Stephen did.

You can have the same ripple effect. The world has never needed it more than now.

CHAPTER 12:

Leader #2 Krista Todd

Now we will look at a leader who is humble, caring, and inspirational. Krista Todd is the Chief Marketing Officer (CMO) of NortonLifeLock. When she speaks with you, there is always a spark of connection. She can make you feel as if the whole world stopped, and her attention is just on you—even in the middle of a critical media fiasco. She began in marketing communications and is now a Chief Marketing Officer.

LEADER #2: KRISTA TODD, CHIEF MARKETING OFFICER (CMO) FOR NORTONLIFELOCK

VOLLEYBALL AND LEADERSHIP

Bump. Set. Spike. The player who spikes the ball over the net for the kill shot receives most of the glory and accolades on the volleyball court.

For Krista, her favorite position was the setter. In this role, she could be behind-the-scenes and still lead.

Many don't know this, but the setter is running the play. Krista loved the subtlety of how she could be the one bringing up other people and putting them in a position to shine. As a setter, she was the second player to touch the ball every play. You need to put the ball in the best place so the hitters can make the most out of the play.

On the volleyball court she began to learn lessons of leadership, which she now recognizes. Similar to being a setter in volleyball, you have to have the right players in the right roles at the right time working on the right projects to have things come together. This is one of the core philosophies of how she led her team as the Head of Global Comms at Logitech and now as CMO at NortonLifeLock.

Look at where you have your employees positioned. Are they in the right places for the organization and the projects? Just as importantly, are they in the right positions for where they want to be and where they can grow the most?

DON'T HESITATE TO ASK

When she was twenty-four years old, Krista joined the Communications and Public Relations team at TiVo. The team only had three people when she started. However, the number quickly changed. Within sixty days, the director left for Apple. Then the VP moved to Los Angeles. Their three-person team was now Krista.

"Why don't you let me try to lead?" Krista offered. "I'm going to report to a CMO, anyway. Let me lead the communications team and report to the CMO for a bit. I know I can help."

For her, leadership has been saying yes and taking on the unknown. She had belief in herself, raised her hand, and inspired others to believe in her. She was confident and humble enough to ask others for the help she needed.

Now, as a CMO, she leans into asking questions even more. For example, she knows she doesn't know more than the government affairs lead who has been in the position for twenty-five years. That said, she knows the right questions to ask. Krista believes in admitting to the things you don't know.

Other leaders feel like they have to know everything. They are defensive and guarded. Krista is honest with herself and others. In being authentic with the CEO (her manager) and her team, she has built a solid connection with them.

Krista models creating a culture of curiosity, which enables others to be more open with her. She does not need to have all the answers because she respects the knowledge and experience of her team.

In asking questions to understand and showing respect for others and their expertise, you can create a safe environment for your team to voice their opinions without hesitation.

As an employee, don't hesitate to ask to take on the next big role or project or small step that moves you to where you want to go. When in the new role, connect with others and leverage their experience. Be the part of creating a culture of curiosity by asking questions.

As a manager in a new role, connecting with others is crucial to leading well. As Krista modeled, you are showing respect for the expertise, and you can gain alignment for your vision and roadmap by creating allies.

BELIEF BECOMES ENGAGEMENT

Building on the idea of putting the right people in the right roles at the right time, Krista always believes in finding ways to help people continue to grow.

As an executive, she views one of her responsibilities as knowing her team well. She thinks of her team in this way:

- What are their responsibilities today?
- What are their areas of growth?
- Where are they passionate?
- What can they do in twelve, eighteen, or twenty-four months?

In some ways, it is like a chess game. She considers how she can give her people access to a variety of projects to round them out. The more exposure you can get people across an organization, the more likely they are to want to keep growing and growing with the company.

At another tech company, Krista saw Juliette, a rising star, was starting to plateau and would want more growth. Krista immediately thought of Juliette when she heard there would be a big holiday campaign on the digital acquisition team, a growth team, that would need EMEA support to make the campaign global—optimization for the market as well as localization.

"Give Juliette the role," Krista said to Paolo, who was in charge of the EMEA team.

They carved out the project for her. Krista and Juliette also discussed what Juliette would need to give up in her current role to be able to run the entire holiday campaign effectively. They collaborated on what the role should be. That way, they had clear boundaries in place, and they set the expectations. Juliette loved working on the campaign, and it was a great success. She was very engaged.

This example shows the importance of several of the bricks. Krista and Juliette had already established a solid foundation in those first eighteen months of working together. Krista believed in Juliette and what she could do. In setting clear expectations and boundaries, Krista enabled Juliette to be successful, which further strengthened the bridge.

By creating a strong foundation and showing belief in your employee, they will often exceed your expectations, be engaged, and become loyal. When providing opportunities for your team, define the expectations and boundaries with them so that they are part of the creation, which will help them feel more empowered as well as more engaged.

WHAT COMES AROUND GOES AROUND—IN THE BEST WAY

While still at Logitech, they tapped Krista for a short-term role, which would round out her marketing experience as well.

Scott Wharton, who runs the Video Conferencing (VC) group, needed someone to step in as his head of marketing was moving into another role. His team was going through a bit of transition at the time.

"I just need someone to run marketing for a bit," he said.

"I have a job. I'm running all of global comms, Scott."

After a moment of consideration, she asked, "What would it involve, Scott?"

"I just need someone who understands the business, understands marketing, and understands storytelling. We need to look at the organizational structure. We also need to take a closer look at the strategy and vision for marketing. Then we need to evolve the culture," he explained.

"I can do those things," she said.

Krista and Scott discussed what it would look like if she came on to help. She wanted the role to be temporary, as she loved her head of global communications role. The fact that she didn't have vast experience or knowledge in marketing didn't deter her. She knew the video conferencing business, storytelling, and how to create a great team and great culture. She knew she had a solid team in her Global

Comms team, and this opportunity to work with Scott would also enable some of the leaders in the comms team a chance to step up and step into roles that would round them out as well.

After they aligned on the expectations for the six-month role, Krista dove into it. She found being uncomfortable can be okay. She was more likely to take risks.

This new project ultimately gave her the confidence to move from the Head of Global Communications at Logitech to the CMO role where she is now. She currently works for the former CFO of Logitech, who is now the CEO of NortonLifeLock. Building up the relationship with him opened the door to this new role with a solid bridge already in place.

Because Krista had built a strong relationship with Scott, they both had mutual trust in and respect for each other. They collaborated well and had a solid connection. This is why Scott thought of her for the position and, in part, how she was able to excel and take risks in the position. Scott believed in her the same way she believed in her team. She, like Stephen, has created leaders who have positive ripple effects on others.

CONNECTION THROUGH QUESTIONS
When Krista started at NortonLifeLock, she wanted to know more about her leadership team. She did what most executives do, and she told them about her. Then she added a twist. She had them answer some questions and discuss them with her to know them well.

Some questions were as you might expect:

- What are the three things I should know about you?
- What's the best way to communicate with you?
- How do you like to receive feedback?

Some questions were different from what you might expect:

- What irritates you?
- How can I get a gold star from you?

From this information, Krista modifies how she manages the individuals on her leadership team, as discussed in the Connection chapter. She personalizes her leadership style to them. It really is *one size fits you* leadership style. Then as she works with them, she confirms the answers they provided line up with her experiences of them. In doing this, she knows she may need to follow up with someone within a week before they go too far astray or that another person really likes public feedback and accolades.

If a team member prefers direct, timely feedback, which is straightforward and shared with context, when she has the conversation, she reminds them that is what they shared. If delivering the feedback in this way doesn't work for them, they can communicate back preferences. This is a great example of how the bridge is always a two-way bridge. For the bridge to be solid, both sides need to communicate well, listen effectively, ask questions, and seek to understand the other well.

Preferences evolve and are dynamic, so having regular check-ins on style, preference, etc., is a good thing. For example, if someone shares that they give a gold star to those who collaborate well, it is important to showcase that behavior regularly and ask for feedback on collaboration to confirm if you are meeting their expectations.

With transparency, she often asks: "Is there anything else you wanted to know or were expecting to hear that you haven't heard yet?"

With Krista's personalized leadership style, we can see *one size fits you* modeled effectively. By adjusting her style to match their communication style and needs, Krista has a very engaged team with low turnover. She works consistently and intentionally to build trust, respect, and connection with all of her team. Leveraging these examples, you can create a solid bridge with your team as well.

Leverage the questions Krista offered and add your own to know your team and understand what drives and inspires them.

CHAPTER 13:

Leader #3 Rodney Toy

Now let's look at a thirty-year tech veteran who has held a number of executive positions and is currently an adviser who specializes in go-to-market, revenue, and sales operations. He is a natural connector with genuine care to develop people. Even though I never worked directly for Rodney, I gravitated to him as a mentor, as many did. His door was always open to talk about where you wanted to grow in your career and as a person. Over the years, he is one whose advice I have sought for career, management, and leadership advice.

LEADER #3: RODNEY TOY, TECH EXECUTIVE AND ADVISER

Just out of college and working his first professional job, Rodney was having dinner with eight of his close friends, all of whom worked in different industries. One by one, they talked about the past week at work.

"He was such a jerk today. He nitpicked about everything," said Jodi, Rodney's friend who worked in retail.

"Yea. My boss was so frustrating today. Nothing could go right," said Jeff, a program manager.

After finishing a story about his day, James, who worked in tech, concluded with, "This job is pretty awesome. I like the people and the team I work with. They are supportive, and we all seem to get along. Our manager lets us do our thing."

As they described their experiences, Rodney came to a realization that changed his outlook on management forever. Their perception of how their days went inevitably seemed to focus on interactions they had with their manager that day. If they'd had positive interactions with their manager, it was a great day. With negative interactions, it was a crummy day. While it wasn't the only thing that mattered, the interaction with their managers seemed to be the driving force behind their outlook more times than not.

Maybe you have had similar experiences. I know I have. Of the numerous managers I have had over my twenty years in the corporate world, only a few have stood out that were good at managing. Good or not so great, they all had a huge impact on my day. They all taught me lessons on how I wanted to manage as well. Some lessons were about how to manage, and some were about how not to manage.

Rodney realized early in his career that being a manager was a privilege and not a right—and also a massive responsibility because of the potential to have such a large impact on someone's day—as well as directly impact their physical and mental health, their interactions with their family outside of work, and their overall outlook. He understood how important it was to have a great relationship with your manager, which was exactly how he wanted to manage.

~ ~ ~ ~

Rodney had an incredible internal business partner, Dennis, who saw great things in him early on. He later plucked him out of Finance and moved him into Sales. Rodney learned many of his management lessons from being under Dennis's wing.

THE ART OF THE HIGH FIVE
Dennis walked the halls of his sales organization every morning. Even as a senior executive in the company, Dennis knew everyone's name in the sales organization. He made it a point to smile and say hello to everyone, and often as he passed by, he would give them a high five.

"What have you sold today? Or how's your day going?" he'd call out jovially before pausing to speak with each person.

The first question was not really about what they had actually sold. The question was an icebreaker to chat and therefore build on their connection.

Similar to chats my grandfather would have as he walked around the mill each morning, Dennis was connecting with his people. He was doing it in his own authentic way. In part, Dennis connected with them because he, like my grandfather, was gregarious. Even more than that, both were genuine with what they were doing. They wanted to build the relationship.

Dennis did this up and down his organization—not just with those he interacted with on a regular basis.

Often, senior executives spend most of their time with other senior executives, walking past employees in the company without even saying hello to acknowledge them. By knowing their names, a little bit about their families, or their passions, he made it a point to make everyone feel valued, seen, and critical to the success of the company—not just his most senior team members and managers.

Rodney blended this into his management and continues to walk the halls and talk to people to this day. Dennis and Rodney share the view that employees are people, not assets. Rodney cares about their dreams, their families, and their livelihood.

In connecting this way, people know you genuinely care and want to know about them. They feel valued. An additional benefit is this enables you to find out what is happening and any challenges the team or organization may be facing. When people feel valued and heard, they speak up more often and more openly.

PLAYING DUMBO COLOMBO AND THE ART OF ORCHESTRATION

Dennis had a knack for leading people to the answer without telling them what to do. Rodney called it "playing Dumbo Colombo," a reference to the seventies hit show *Colombo* starring Peter Falk. Peter was an unassuming homicide detective who would ask seemingly simple questions to tease out answers.

Before meetings, Rodney and Dennis would always often confer and strategize.

"Here's what we want to get out of the meeting," Dennis would start.

Then they would discuss what was important about the outcome for the meeting and also who would be in attendance at the meeting, what their viewpoints on the issues were likely going to be and strategize on how to orchestrate the meeting in such a way to achieve the desired outcomes by building consensus from the team.

At one point in their tenure working together, Dennis was the CEO of a publicly traded company, and Rodney was his primary lieutenant. While both had strong backgrounds in sales and marketing, neither had worked in engineering and they were now responsible for technical teams. Though neither was very technical, they both had a gut for what needed to happen, and they were open to what the engineers would propose. They would both listen as the engineers discussed an issue.

"Listen, guys, I'm not technical, so forgive me if this is a dumb question," Dennis would say before asking a question.

Often Dennis knew what he wanted the outcome to be, and he would just lead the team to the place they needed to go. By Dennis leveraging this technique of asking *basic questions*, the team felt heard and valued. Often, the team would improve on the outcome Dennis had originally envisioned because the team felt like they had a say in the decision, and he created a culture of curiosity. The team felt empowered to suggest changes and improvements. Some may have misconstrued this as indecisiveness, but it was not. Dennis was able to make definitive and often hard decisions when needed. However, when he could afford to do so, which was often, he chose this approach.

As Rodney watched, this happened again and again. He noticed Dennis had this patient demeanor about him. He didn't have an ego, as some executives did, where he had to give the answer and have everyone else follow. While some executives prefer to come in and bark the answer, Dennis had a different default method. Rodney is the first to admit sometimes this method might result in another meeting, and he felt it was worth the time. This was playing the long game because this created trust, respect, and connection.

When you let go of your ego, you can create stronger relationships. Investing the time to reinforce the connection with the team always pays off. You can grow trust by empowering your team to own their roles more. The leader's role is to let them drive the car while ensuring they stay on the road and head in the right direction. Enabling your employee to make the decisions and allowing them the opportunity to figure out the best path provides them with the support they need to grow. This is the belief that we highlighted earlier, and with this, employees feel more confident, valued, and respected, which enables them to show up even more.

ALWAYS "WE" NOT "YOU"
Rodney never had to worry about his place with his manager, Dennis. He created a safe environment for Rodney to be put

into these roles that Rodney was not on paper qualified for. He moved him into his first Vice President (VP) role before he had the number of years of experience that others had.

"Don't worry. I have you," Dennis said to Rodney.

With that assurance, Rodney never worried about Dennis judging him. Rodney felt he could ask Dennis any question, even if it sounded basic in his mind. They discussed all the situations and challenges that a new VP would have.

This belief from Dennis created a safe environment where Rodney was given the opportunity to succeed and to learn from any missteps. Because of this safe environment, Rodney could approach Dennis with these questions without feeling nervous.

- "I don't know how to handle this person. What would you recommend?"
- "I need to fire this person. What do I do?"

Dennis became more than his manager. He also became a mentor. He always used "we" and not "you." This instilled a sense of "we're in this together" for Rodney. Dennis taught Rodney about the importance of investing time in making sure he was successful. Because of this investment—the trust, the opportunities, and their connection—Rodney showed up in a bigger way for Dennis. They became a great duo. Their communication and connection were so cohesive Rodney could read the room and take signals from Dennis without Dennis saying anything directly to him.

Later, Rodney poured these same investments into others—some on his team and some not.

DEVELOPING PEOPLE IS A TWO-WAY ENDEAVOR
At a different organization, Rodney had incredible conversations with an employee within his organization who wanted to develop her career. While she did not work directly for him, Rodney always instituted an open-door policy. She approached him about her plan for the future. Sometimes people expect the manager to lay out a plan for them if they want to be promoted. They "make the mistake of sitting back and waiting for others" to plan for them, Rodney told me over lunch.

Kristin was different. She proactively put together a career development plan. She scheduled quarterly meetings with Rodney and diligently followed up on the action items they had agreed on in their prior meeting and came prepared with questions and asks to discuss with Rodney. This demonstrated her commitment, showed her initiative, and made it easy for Rodney to support her.

I'm not saying you have to map out exactly what you want and the activities. That is not what she did. She came with a rough plan that addressed what she felt were the pieces she needed to fill in to move to the next level as a starting point for their discussion. It was a collaboration between the two of them, as well as her manager. Rodney worked jointly with her manager to support her goals—such as introducing her to other valuable mentors, getting her training in areas that she had expressed an interest in learning more about, and ensuring she had the internal visibility necessary to support her career development goals. Kristin did not sit on the sidelines and hope someone else would develop a plan for her.

As an employee, know what you want and come with potential solutions. Listen and be open to the feedback of where you have needs to address. Respect the experience of the manager or manager's manager. Build that relationship and rapport. Trust that they believe in you.

Rodney always asks members of his team and most anyone else who would come into his office:

What do you want to be when you grow up? Where do you want to go?

This question isn't only about their career. It's about them—their career plus their life, their dreams, their hopes. This discussion is about supporting their development as a person, with the career being just one component.

He creates a safe space, the same way that Dennis did for him, so they can talk with him about their hopes. He sees each person as the complex, multifaceted human that they are. He offers them guidance on how to get where they want to go. In doing this, people feel valued. That is part of the reason so many people have always wanted to work for him wherever he goes.

This is the power of bringing all the bricks together.

CHAPTER 14:

Final Thoughts

"If only one side builds the bridge, it is a lookout. Both sides are needed to build the bridge."

~KIMBERLY SAUCEDA

Building bridges is more critical now than ever. The relationship of manager to employee and employee to manager is vital for a thriving organization.

Previously, companies would focus solely on the results and not as much on the relationships. That is no longer possible. Maybe it never really was.

In my discussion with Peggy Northrop, CEO of Watermark, we talked about how companies once tried to wring every last drop of productivity out of someone. Being so focused on productivity is like Henry Ford only focusing on optimizing output. This causes burnout. People are not resources. The focus needs to be on the relationship for the well-being of the employee, the manager, their teams, and the company as a whole.

A massive wave of people quit in 2021. According to a 2022 *Fast Company* article citing recent Gallup data, "Two-thirds of the reasons people actually left jobs in 2021 were due to issues related to their engagement and their overall well-being."

Sometimes both managers and employees say their problems are "too big" or that they "cannot have an impact" on them.

"What can *I* do to impact burnout?"

"Employees need to advocate for themselves. As a manager, I cannot change things. I am only one part of this big machine."

We have seen the impact of burnout, decline in employee engagement, and challenges with overwork. These impact the employees and managers. Then there are also the financial costs these impacts have on organizations.

Yet, we have also seen throughout this book the impact managers and employees can also have when they build the bridge together.

To begin the process of building the bridge, we start with trust, respect, and connection. You need a solid foundation from which to start or everything else breaks down.

Trust is the cornerstone we start with and is learnable, as Stephen M.R. Covey pointed out in his book *Speed of Trust*.

Creating trust between employee and manager enables you both to reap the benefits of the High Trust Dividends. Through having an open and transparent dialogue, trust deepens.

Trust without respect is not enough. Think about it like a garden. Both sunshine and watering are necessary for the garden to grow and blossom to its fullest. Respect leads to more engagement and healthier teams. Understand your organization, its values, your values, and the values of your employee. Then find the right balance of owed respect (that universal need to feel included) and earned respect (recognition of valued qualities or behaviors). Both are necessary.

Connection is the glue that holds this foundation together. People have always wanted to be seen and heard. Whether you are remote, in person, or hybrid, connection ties us together. Actions—like giving out high fives, having a coffee klatch, or checking in to see how people are truly doing—build a deeper sense of connection. Show you genuinely care and help them know you will be there for them. Create your personalized management style—the one that works for you with each of your team members.

One of my favorite things to do with my team was a walking one-on-one. We would take the one-on-one outside. Each would begin with checking in on how they were—not just at work but overall in life. Then we would discuss their projects, their challenges, as well as their latest accomplishments. This is an easy way to build trust and connection. Even if you are remote, you can both still walk and discuss.

Each day, in small and big ways, it is about continuing to strengthen the relationship by reinforcing the bridge. If you are doing these steps in small ways each day, when something comes up (as it always does), you can count on the other person, your manager or your employee, to be there. You are not scrambling to fix the relationship.

Setting expectations, gaining alignment, and believing in your employee or manager are the three key tools for strengthening the bridge.

Setting expectations between employee and manager will help you each to be on the same page. What is right for both of you? There will be times when this needs flex—when things are busy at work or when work is lighter. Define what boundaries are important for you. Then discuss them and follow through on them. With no lines between work and personal, this is as important for your mental health as it is for relationship building.

Gaining alignment keeps both sides in sync with each other. Choose how to best align on your goals and next steps, knowing each other's motivations and expectations.

The crux of all great relationships in my interviews and research was developing others and being a partner in their development. This is where great leaders light up when talking about managing and where great employees that love their managers light up as well. It is almost a magical piece that comes from a marriage of belief in someone and a growth mindset. It is in empowering the employee and stepping up into that responsibility of being empowered and then over-delivering.

All of this takes care and intention. In the world of remote, hybrid, or in-person environments, taking the time to have consistent, intentional actions will strengthen these relationships.

Sometimes, even with the best of intentions, relationships have challenges. It is important to maintain or rebuild the bridge. If these challenges occur, focus on curiosity, actively listening, and ownership with consistency.

In asking open-ended questions, which start with what or how, you can better understand each other and what is important. Often, conflict can stem from a misunderstanding or lack of communication about what is important for each party.

If you are a manager, have the conversation and offer ideas of what you can do and explore what your employee can do, again leveraging how and what questions or the incredible "how might we" question.

When listening, remember to tap into the Level Two and Level Three listening skills to understand what the other person is communicating, including their nonverbal cues. These key coaching skills can completely change your relationship.

Ownership with consistency along with curiosity and listening rebuilds the bridge. Owning your part in the deterioration and then acting consistently to rebuild it is key.

Finally, loop back to the first foundation: trust, respect, and connection. With these, the initial foundation is created.

When things fall apart, you need to own your part and then rebuild trust, respect, and connection. Without this, it is not possible to move forward with the relationships.

Bridges need to be maintained and reinforced so they do not atrophy and break down.

CONSISTENT BRIDGE BUILDING LEADS TO LONG-LASTING LOYALTY

Nick was Head of Tax at a medium-sized wine shipping company. Just after a challenging season with tax returns, he took his team and some partners to Alpha Omega Winery, where they enjoyed a relaxing afternoon tour of the winery. His team was a very close-knit group. They shared joys with each other and bonded together. When Nick needed to call on them to work a bit more, they would chip in and do more than their part.

He had built this camaraderie through acts of appreciation in a variety of ways—regular feedback, boba tea runs, etc. He looked out for each of them by highlighting their efforts to management. They were so close they teared up when Nick announced he would be leaving to go to another organization. A decade later, he still has people from this team ask to work for him.

~ ~ ~ ~

We know from the Great Resignation and Gallup's research published in the March 2022 *Fast Company* article noted above that 42 percent of the people who quit in 2021 cited reasons tied to how they felt about their bosses and organizational cultures. This is something that both sides can change—as a manager and as an employee.

I hope you will leverage all the bricks in the chapters of this book and build solid relationships that create healthy, high-performing teams with happy managers and employees. When we start with the focus on creating solid relationships, this is the world of work in which we will all thrive. This is where organizations thrive and produce great results.

By putting all these bricks together, you will see the strongest relationships and the best results.

Acknowledgments

This book is only possible because of the love and support of so many phenomenal people—my family, friends, colleagues, mentors, fellow coaches, and authors. Writing a book is a massive undertaking. I am so grateful to all of those who have supported me along this journey.

First, my family...

To my sweet husband, Carlos, thank you for being an amazing support system and always encouraging me to chase after my dreams. You are an incredible partner and friend. *To Andrew,* you were truly the inspiration for this book and the bridge. Thank you for being a great bridge builder and for helping me talk my thoughts through. Who knows, maybe you will write a book one day. *To Lucas,* you are the best behind-the-scenes hype machine. From helping with video creation to daily support, you are the sweetest. I love you 3000 and all the way beyond the moon.

To my mama, thank you for being such an amazing role model. You have reinvented what you want to do a few times, setting a great example for me that anything is truly achievable. You've always told me to go after my dreams. It turns out encouraging my love of analogies and metaphor has paid off. Extra shout out for being a very thorough editor.

To my dad, your support and guidance always steadies me in times of turmoil. I appreciate all of our chats and your love more than you will ever know.

To Nana and Papa, who first taught me how to lead from the front, from behind, and from the side—as well as the power of genuinely caring for and connecting to others. I cherish all the lessons you taught me, especially those while baking and those in the sawmill.

To Kathi, one of the best bridge builders in the business world, thank you for believing in me and offering your support and guidance along the way.

To Matt, you are my rock. I love that I can call anytime, and you always know the right thing to say… and you brought back my favorite drink. You truly are my favorite brother. Ich liebe dich.

To Christian, my close-enough-to-be-a-brother best friend, thank you for reminding me to "hit the nails first and take care of the other things later." This is not only great book writing advice, but incredible life advice. Kind of like the advice you would give chasing thunderstorms in the Ford Fairlane.

To Lisa, my close-enough-to-be-a-sister best friend, thank you for always having my back and loving me in the fiercest way. You were my first bridge.

To my incredible friends that read the entire book...

To Monique Relova, first thank you for being such a great friend over the years. We have discussed several iterations of this book, and it would not be as good as it is without you and your wisdom. Your help and guidance have been there at every critical moment, even during the name brainstorm.

To Jenny Scothorn, my friend for more than two decades. Thank you for the truss idea. I promise I am leveraging it in my leadership development program that is coming straight from this book. I appreciate your insights for what to keep, what to highlight, what to let go. All of it has been so helpful.

To Bill Carmody, who consistently nudged me about writing this book each time we spoke, telling me that you knew I had a book inside of me that the world would want to hear, maybe even two. Thank you so much for your ideas and words of wisdom.

To Michelle, my talented friend who originally inspired this book over swirls during one of our many conversations about how to change the world one leader at a time. I owe you another swirl or two.

To Ann Farrell, who consistently leads with a big heart and has always seen something in me before I see it. This book may be one of the biggest surprises I didn't fully see coming, my friend. Thank you for never-ending belief. My life is forever changed.

To my editors...

To *Karina Agbisit*, my developmental editor, who worked with me to develop this book. In a crazy moment in November, when we made a pivot, you were there for me every step of the way, with words of encouragement and ideas for what to do next. This book would just be an idea without you.

To *Sandy Huffman*, my fearless revisions editor, who helped me hone the rough draft of this book into a book that I am very proud of. I could not have asked for a better person to run to the finish line with. You are a beautiful mix of wittiness, wicked good editor chops, the ability to give feedback from the heart, and solid instinct to know when I need a nudge and when I need encouragement. I appreciate our chats, brainstorms, and gossip sessions about pop culture. Thank you for having my book editing feel like it was as important to you as it is to me. Thank you for understanding why a book cover image matters so much.

I interviewed dozens and dozens of people for this book. Several would prefer not to be named. Whether named or not, this book is much stronger because of the stories included from those interviews. Thank you to everyone who spent time with me to discuss what creates a strong bridge.

To *Stephen Bohnet,* who truly is a unicorn of a manager, even if he does not see himself that way. You set a high bar for others. I learned so much about being a great leader from you. I am forever grateful for those lessons, the camping, and our enduring connection.

To Krista Todd, they broke the mold after you. So many people love working with you. I did consider switching to PR just to work more closely with you. I love how you model every day how to build trust and respect and how to lift up other women leaders. I'm so grateful (and blessed) that we have remained friends.

To Rodney Toy, the mentor and adviser I have called before any big career decision. Thank you for always having an open door, listening, and fully hearing me. Your guidance has been invaluable. I appreciate how you give so much back to the world and grow leaders, inside and out of the departments you lead.

To Jennifer Moss, thank you for giving your time to chat with me about my book and how burnout is affecting all levels. You are a talented author, and I feel blessed to have you in my circle.

To Jennifer Britton, I have learned so much from you about leading and motivating from our chats and your book. I appreciate you sharing them with me to include in my book, especially the CLAIMS model.

Last but certainly not least, some amazing friends and thought partners who helped me throughout this book writing journey and even before.

To Andy Pray, you are an inspirational leader. I loved our conversation, your vulnerability, your introspection... I hope we continue to have more conversations.

To Derek Gordon, with the best laugh that always makes me smile. Thank you for modeling what great leadership looks like for me early in my career.

To Peggy Northrop, thank you for the many insights about how the world has been changing and what it takes to be a great leader today.

To Liyani Rodriguez, thank you for your support and for leveraging your company to help me create the best book title. Your greatness has ripples.

To Steve Sinclair, thank you for teaching me about boundaries and how important they are.

To Charles Sue-Wah-Sing, for the metaphors, imagery, and rich discussions. You are a true sage and a wonderful friend.

To Aaron, who has become a great friend. Your stories and insight were so helpful. Those who work with, for, around, and near you are the luckiest. You have an incredible ability to listen and really hear others.

To Alex, thank you for the numerous coffee chats at Philz where we covered everything from book covers to chapter names. I always appreciate your opinions and thoughts.

To Christopher, thank you for our many virtual chats on everything from Leadership to trust to witsec. Cheers to being published authors.

To Collette, for the guidance through my most recent career twists and turns and all of the guidance as I wrote this book.

To Erin, for the many leadership discussions over glasses of wine. I'm so glad that our kids met so long ago.

To MK, who helped me sort through how to look at things differently for this book and was my partner in crime for eighteen months. I miss meandering through the hill and dale with you to discuss leadership styles and how to work with different leaders.

To Nick, for the long chat about leadership over coffee on what builds connection and what can destroy it.

To Theresa, for the great discussion on how to rebuild the bridge with intention.

To Tiffany, who brainstormed ideas, topics, stories, marketing, and everything in between over everything from cocktails to coffee. I am grateful for your advice.

To Jen and CJ, my forever CTI carpenter friends, who have my back through whatever may come up.

Appendix

CHAPTER 1:

Barry, Kristin. "Recruiting Women Take More Than Just Competitive Pay." *Gallup*, March 2, 2022. https://www.gallup.com/workplace/390275/recruiting-women-takes-more-than-competitive-pay.aspx.

Birt, Jamie. "92% of COVID Job Switchers Report, 'Life Is Too Short to Stay in a Job You're Not Passionate About'." *Indeed*, December 2, 2021. https://www.indeed.com/career-advice/career-development/covid-job-switching.

Crowley, Mark C. "It's Not Just Money. This Is What's Still Driving the Great Resignation." *Fast Company*, March 5, 2022. https://www.fastcompany.com/90727646/its-not-just-money-this-is-whats-still-driving-the-great-resignation.

Curtin, Melanie. "Employees Who Feel Heard Are 4.6x More Likely to Feel Empowered to Do Their Best Work." *INC,* September 5, 2019. https://www.inc.com/melanie-curtin/employees-who-feel-heard-are-46x-more-likely-to-feel-empowered-to-do-their-best-work.html.

Dimock, Michael. "Defining generations: Where Millennials end and Generation Z begins." *Pew Research Center*, January 17, 2019. https://www.pewresearch.org/fact-tank/2019/01/17/where-millennials-end-and-generation-z-begins/.

Dixon-Fyle, Sundiatu, Kevin Dolan, Vivian Hunt, and Sara Prince. "Diversity Wins and How Inclusion Matters." *McKinsey*, May 19, 2020. https://www.mckinsey.com/featured-insights/diversity-and-inclusion/diversity-wins-how-inclusion-matters.

Foster, Sarah. "Survey: 55% of Americans Expect to Search for a New Job Over the Next 12 Months." *Bankrate*, August 23, 2021. Accessed February 1, 2022. https://www.bankrate.com/personal-finance/job-seekers-survey-august-2021/.

Harter, Jim. "US Employee Engagement Drops for First Year in a Decade." *Gallup*, January 7, 2022. https://www.gallup.com/workplace/388481/employee-engagement-drops-first-year-decade.aspx.

Harter, Jim. "US Employee Engagement Rises Following Wild 2020." *Gallup*, February 26, 2021. https://www.gallup.com/workplace/330017/employee-engagement-rises-following-wild-2020.aspx.

Iacuri, Greg. "4.3 Million People Quit Their Jobs in January as the Great Resignation Shows No Sign of Slowing Down." *CNBC*, March 9, 2022. https://www.cnbc.com/2022/03/09/the-great-resignation-is-still-in-full-swing.html.

Kane, Philip and Grace Ocean. "The Great Resignation Is Here, and It's Real." *INC,* Aug 26, 2021. https://www.inc.com/phillip-kane/the-great-resignation-is-here-its-real.html.

Kropp, Brian and Emily Rose McRad. "11 Trends that Will Shape Work in 2022 and Beyond." *Harvard Business Review,* January 13, 2022. https://hbr.org/2022/01/11-trends-that-will-shape-work-in-2022-and-beyond.

Maslach, Christina and Michael P. Leiter. "Understanding the burnout experience: recent research and its implications for psychiatry" *World Psychiatry* 15, no. 5 (June 2016): 103–111. https://www.ncbi.nlm.nih.gov/pmc/articles/PMC4911781/.

MacNab, Austin. "How Does Inclusive Culture Boost Company Performance?" *Entrepreneur,* February 11, 2022. https://www.entrepreneur.com/article/412820.

Minanhan, Tim. "What Your Future Employees Want Most." *Harvard Business Review,* May 31, 2021. https://hbr.org/2021/05/what-your-future-employees-want-most.

Moss, Jennifer. "Burnout Is About Your Workplace, Not Your People." *Harvard Business Review*, December 11, 2019. https://hbr.org/2019/12/burnout-is-about-your-workplace-not-your-people.

Moss, Jennifer. *The Burnout Epidemic: The Rise of Chronic Stress and How We Can Fix It.*" Boston: Harvard Business Review Press, 2021.

Osborne, Hilary. "Home Workers Putting in More Hours Since COVID, Research Shows." *The Guardian*, February 4, 2021. https://www.theguardian.com/business/2021/feb/04/home-workers-putting-in-more-hours-since-covid-research.

Snyder, Benjamin. "Half of Us Have Quit Our Job Because of a Bad Boss." *Fortune*, April 2, 2015. https://fortune.com/2015/04/02/quit-reasons/.

Society for Human Resource Management. "84% of US Workers Blame Bad Managers for Creating Unnecessary Stress." Society for Human Resource Management press release, August 12, 2020. https://www.shrm.org/about-shrm/press-room/press-releases/pages/survey-84-percent-of-us-workers-blame-bad-managers-for-creating-unnecessary-stress-.aspx.

Tadelis, Steve, and Stephen J. Dubner. "Why Are There So Many Bad Bosses?" March 2, 2022. In *Freakonomics Radio*. Produced by Ryan Kelley. Podcast, MP3 audio, 17:08. https://freakonomics.com/podcast/why-are-there-so-many-bad-bosses/.

Threlkeld, Kristy. "Employee Burnout Report: COVID-19's Impact and 3 Strategies to Curb It." *Indeed*, March 11, 2021. https://www.indeed.com/lead/preventing-employee-burnout-report.

US Department of Labor, Bureau of Labor Statistics. *Job Openings and Labor Turnover Survey News Release*. Washington, DC: January 4, 2022. Accessed February 1, 2022. https://www.bls.gov/news.release/jolts.nr0.htm.

World Health Organization. "Long working Hours Increasing Deaths from Heart Disease and Stroke: WHO, ILO." *World

Health Organization, May 17, 2021. https://www.who.int/news/item/17-05-2021-long-working-hours-increasing-deaths-from-heart-disease-and-stroke-who-ilo.

CHAPTER 2:

Covey, Stephen M.R. *Speed of Trust: The One Thing that Changes Everything.* New York: Simon & Schuster, 2006.

Covey, Stephen M.R. *Trust and Inspire: How Truly Great Leaders Unleash Greatness in Others.* New York: Simon & Schuster, 2021.

Covey, Stephen M.R. "Why Trust Is the Top Requirement for Building and Growing Your Company (and How to Prioritize It)." *Inc.,* October 12, 2021. https://www.inc.com/stephen-m-r-covey/why-trust-is-top-requirement-for-building-growing-your-company-and-how-to-prioritize-it.html.

LEAD. "The Speed of Trust—Stephen M. R. Covey @LEAD Presented by HR.com." April 2016. Video, 25:30. https://www.youtube.com/watch?v=lvlEfNyZ8B0.

Zak, Paul. "The Neuroscience of Trust." *Harvard Business Review,* January 2017. https://hbr.org/2017/01/the-neuroscience-of-trust.

CHAPTER 3:

DeSmet, Aaron, Kim Rubenstein, Gunnar Schrah, Mike Vierow, and Amy Edmondson. "Psychological Safety and Leadership Development" *McKinsey,* February 11, 2021. https://www.mckinsey.com/business-functions/people-and-organizational-performance/our-insights/psychological-safety-and-the-critical-role-of-leadership-development.

Schwartz, Tony, and Christine Porath. "The Power of Meeting Your Employees' Needs." *Harvard Business Review*, June 30, 2014. Accessed May 27, 2022. https://hbr.org/2014/06/the-power-of-meeting-your-employees-needs?registration=success.

CHAPTER 4:

Castrillon, Caroline. "Why 2022 is the Year of Workplace Culture" *Forbes*, December 29, 2021. https://www.forbes.com/sites/carolinecastrillon/2021/12/29/why-2022-is-the-year-of-workplace-culture/?sh=23b24c9a1bbb.

Harter, Jim. "US Employee Engagement Drops for First Year in a Decade." *Gallup*, January 7, 2022. https://www.gallup.com/workplace/388481/employee-engagement-drops-first-year-decade.aspx.

McKay, Jory. "These are 4 styles of communication that you need to know" *Fast Company*. January 25, 2019. https://www.fastcompany.com/90296536/these-are-4-styles-of-communication-that-you-need-to-know.

Smith, Ryan. "How CEOs Can Support Employee Mental Health in Crisis." *Harvard Business Review*, May 1, 2020. https://hbr.org/2020/05/how-ceos-can-support-employee-mental-health-in-a-crisis.

CHAPTER 5:

Abramson, Ashley. "Burnout and Stress are Everywhere." *American Psychological Association* 53 no. 1 (January 2022): 72. https://www.apa.org/monitor/2022/01/special-burnout-stress.

Agovino, Theresa. "The Phenomenon of the Four-Day Workweek" *Society of Human Resource Management*, June 20, 2020. https://www.shrm.org/hr-today/news/all-things-work/pages/four-day-workweek.aspx.

Bartel, Jeffrey. "The Four-Day Workweek Merits Consideration" *Forbes*, May 7, 2021. https://www.forbes.com/sites/forbesfinancecouncil/2021/05/07/the-four-day-workweek-merits-consideration/?sh=a9df86b786dd.

Green, Jeff. "The Pandemic Workday Is 48 Minutes Longer and Has More Meetings." *Bloomberg*, August 3, 2020. https://www.bloomberg.com/news/articles/2020-08-03/the-pandemic-workday-is-48-minutes-longer-and-has-more-meetings.

Kelly, Jack. "The Four-Day Workweek Is Gaining Big Momentum, Signing Up 50 Organizations." *Forbes*, February 3, 2022. https://www.forbes.com/sites/jackkelly/2022/02/03/the-four-day-workweek-is-gaining-big-momentum-signing-up-50-organizations/?sh=597f649c67b6.

Mastroiani, Brian. "Feeling More Stress and Anxiety? Your Smartphone May Be to Blame." *Healthline*, November 13, 2020. https://www.healthline.com/health-news/feeling-more-stress-and-anxiety-your-smartphone-may-be-to-blame.

CHAPTER 7:

Covey, Stephen M.R. *Trust and Inspire: How Truly Great Leaders Unleash Greatness in Others.* New York: Simon & Schuster, 2021.

Dweck, Carol. *Mindset: The New Psychology of Success.* New York: Ballantine Books, 2015.

CHAPTER 8:

Gino, Francesca. "The Business Case for Curiosity." *Harvard Business Review,* September-October 2018. https://hbr.org/2018/09/the-business-case-for-curiosity.

Milway, Katie Smith and Alex Goldmark. "Four Ways to Cultivate a Culture of Curiosity" *Harvard Business Review,* September 13, 2013. https://hbr.org/2013/09/four-ways-to-cultivate-a-culture-of-curiosity.

CHAPTER 9:

Kimsey-House, Henry and Karen Kimsey-House, Phillip Sandahl, and Laura Whitworth. *Co-Active Coaching: The Proven Framework for Transformative Conversations at Work and in Life.* Boston: Nicholas Brealey Publishing, 2005.

TED. "Sheila Heen: How to Use Others' Feedback to Learn and Grow." June 22, 2015. Video, 19:28. https://www.youtube.com/watch?v=FQNbaKkYk_Q.

CHAPTER 10:

Caza, Brianna Barker, Mara Olekans, and Timothy Vogus. "How to Mend a Work Relationship" *Harvard Business Review*, February 14, 2020. https://hbr.org/2020/02/how-to-mend-a-work-relationship.

CHAPTER 14:

Covey, Stephen M.R. *Speed of Trust: The One Thing that Changes Everything.* New York: Simon & Schuster, 2006.

Crowley, Mark C. "It's Not Just Money. This Is What's Still Driving the Great Resignation" *Fast Company*, March 5, 2022. https://www.fastcompany.com/90727646/its-not-just-money-this-is-whats-still-driving-the-great-resignation.

CPSIA information can be obtained
at www.ICGtesting.com
Printed in the USA
LVHW030501110922
728012LV00001B/3